THE
BERRIGAN
BROTHERS

THE BERRIGAN BROTHERS

The Story of
Daniel and Philip Berrigan

RICHARD CURTIS

HAWTHORN BOOKS, INC.
Publishers/NEW YORK

Title page photo: United Press International Photo

ACKNOWLEDGMENT

My deepest appreciation to Tom Robbins,
whose aid on this project was invaluable

THE
BERRIGAN
BROTHERS

1

On a warm and sunny afternoon in Catonsville, Maryland, on May 17, 1968, three cars pulled into the parking lot beside the Knights of Columbus Hall. A small group of reporters and television cameramen who had been standing at one end of the lot watched as seven men and two women emerged from the cars. Two of the men carried large wire-mesh trash baskets. Together they walked to the entrance of the hall and ascended to the second-floor office of the local board of the Selective Service System.

Three women were sitting at desks sorting through papers and typing letters. Without speaking, five of the visitors entered the office and crossed to the file cabinets where the draft records were stored. Throwing open the drawers, they began snatching up handfuls of papers and stuffing them into the baskets. For a moment the three clerks watched in stunned silence. Then the head clerk jumped up from her desk. "My files, my files!" she screamed. Grabbing one of the baskets, she attempted to pull it out of the hands of a raider. She was gently but firmly pushed aside. Another clerk threw a telephone through a nearby window in an effort to gain the attention of passersby. The raiders worked quickly, shouting words of encouragement to each other.

In less than two minutes the baskets were filled. The nine intruders rushed from the office and down the stairs to the parking lot outside. There, the baskets were emptied onto the macadam pavement. Two bottles, containing a

3

homemade version of napalm, were produced and poured over the pile. Matches were lit and hurled onto the heap. With a sharp roar, it burst into flames.

The nine raiders stepped back, smiled, and congratulated one another. None of them made any attempt to flee the scene of the crime. Arms crossed in front of them, they held hands in a circle and began reciting the Lord's Prayer.

The reporters, who had been summoned and escorted to the demonstration by companions of the raiders, ripped open the sealed envelopes they had been given earlier in the day. A statement was enclosed:

> Today, May 17th, we enter Local Board number 33 at Catonsville, Maryland, to seize Selective Service records and burn them with napalm. . . . We are Catholic Christians who take our faith seriously. We use napalm because it has burned people to death in Vietnam, Guatemala and Peru and because it may be used in American ghettos. We destroyed these records because they exploit our young men and represent misplaced power concentrated in the hands of the ruling class. . . . We believe some property has no right to exist.

For people who had just violated several federal laws, and stood liable to severe jail sentences, they were an odd-looking group. All dressed neatly and conservatively, three of the men wore clerical collars. Two of these were brothers.

Philip Berrigan, the leader of the raid and a priest in the order of Saint Joseph, stood with his head slightly bowed toward the fire, a solemn look on his face. Despite graying hair, his tall and massive body gave the impression of great physical power as though he were a prizefighter turned priest. Beside him stood his brother, Daniel. Shorter and thinner than Philip, Daniel Berrigan wore a slight grin on his gaunt face, his mouth just barely turning up at the corners. A priest in the Society of Jesus (known as the Jesuits), he stood very much at ease in the small circle as the prayer was recited.

May, 1968, found the nation and the world in great turmoil. The war in Vietnam, although undeclared as an official war by the U.S. government, was consuming hundreds of lives each day. Five hundred sixty-two Americans and over five thousand Vietnamese had died in the week preceding the raid on the Catonsville draft board—the highest figures recorded since the war had begun. Although Dean Rusk, the Secretary of State, had declared a year earlier that he could "see the light at the end of the tunnel," the war continued to consume more and more lives and lay waste ever-widening areas of Vietnamese soil. Even those Americans who had supported the entrance of the United States into the conflict were finding if difficult to comprehend the terrible and seemingly endless costs of the war. And a growing number of people were finding themselves firmly opposed to American involvement in all its moral and legal aspects.

In October, 1967, a demonstration by over one hundred thousand people from across the country was held in Washington, D.C., to protest the war. President Lyndon Johnson ordered the 82nd Airborne Division to the city to protect government buildings as marchers gathered in front of the Pentagon and the White House to "confront the warmakers." In Oakland, California, thousands of protesters filled the streets surrounding the Bay Area induction center, stopping all traffic and refusing to allow the draft processing to continue. On dozens of college campuses, students angry over the war and the presence of reserve officer training programs on campus, seized buildings and called for boycotts of classes. At Columbia University, San Francisco State College, Harvard, Berkeley, the University of Wisconsin, and many other schools there were violent clashes between

5

police and students. Newspapers began to speak of "the great division in American Society," as dissent increased and the war continued to escalate.

For many Americans the barbarism of the Vietnam war became a mirror image of life in America itself. Those who were appalled at photographs of Vietnamese children scarred and disfigured by the burns of napalm dropped from American warplanes began to question the entire nature of a society that could produce such horror.

At the end of World War II American society had begun an earnest pursuit of the "American Dream" that had eluded it during the long Depression and the years of war. Exactly what this "dream" consisted of was vague, but it seemed to imply such things as two cars in the garage, television in the bedroom as well as the parlor, and meat on the table seven nights a week. In short, it was a life of modest luxury and leisure.

That such a life was far beyond the means of the great majority of Americans did not stop politicians and advertisers from tantalizingly dangling it before the eyes of the people. Everything from deodorants to automobiles was pictured as a necessary item to have along on the road to success and happiness. Television quiz shows offered a crack at instant fortune to lucky contestants who could answer a simple question correctly, while millions of viewers looked on envyingly.

In schools the American way of life was pictured as being second to none, promising an abundance of riches and freedom for everyone. As an enormous number of products swelled the market each year, many Americans became accustomed to credit buying: a plan that enabled them to enjoy an expensive item without having the money to pay for it. For many, credit buying became a way of life, as television commercials constantly hammered away at them with orders of "Be the first!" or "Don't be the only one without . . ."

Toward the end of the nineteen-fifties the results of this relentless pursuit of the "dream" began coming into focus. A number of quiz shows were discovered to be rigged and their contestants to have been coached. The increase in American manufacturing in the postwar boom had resulted in the pollution of rivers and lakes. The cities, because of the thousands of cars that clogged the streets each working day, were shrouded in a bad-smelling haze and a new word, "smog," came into use. Nor did affluence help to heal the problems of middle-class families. The divorce rate rose immensely in the years following the war, and young people, who were supposed to be the main recipients of an easier and more relaxed life, began to feel themselves pushed into a way of life they were not sure they understood or desired. To the anguish of their parents, many young, middle-class whites took heavily to the use of drugs in an effort to tranquilize themselves against the pressures they felt.

And there were millions of Americans who had been left far behind in the race toward affluence. Black people, despite government legislation and Supreme Court decisions aimed at improving their conditions, remained excluded from decent jobs, education, and housing. Throughout the Deep South and clustered in the rundown sections of northern and midwestern cities, black people were a major exception to the glowing portraits of American life. Their attempts at organizing a movement that could fight for social change were met by fire hoses and police dogs in Birmingham and billy clubs and bombs in Selma.

As America moved into the sixties, the frustration of both those who could not capture the "dream" and those who had attained a part of it, was growing. As the events of

1967 and 1968 unrolled there seemed a certain irony in President Johnson's proclamation that "we must always remember that our foreign policy is simply a reflection of our policies at home."

On April 4, 1968, in Memphis, Tennessee, the Reverend Martin Luther King, Jr., the most heralded leader of the black movement for equality, was shot dead. King's credo had been nonviolence, the method of Gandhi in India and Jesus of Nazareth before him. The tragic irony of King's violent death was like a spark in a tinder-dry forest. In dozens of cities across America, riots erupted as black people took to the streets to vent their rage and fury. In downtown Washington the entire city seemed in flames as billowing smoke rose from every direction. In newspapers around the country a remarkable photograph was published. Three grim-faced soldiers were shown squatting behind a machinegun position on the steps of the Capitol. The terror and the violence of the Vietnam war was coming home.

In Chicago, Senator Robert F. Kennedy, a candidate for the Democratic nomination for President, went into the cordoned-off section of the city during the height of the riots to plead for peace with the residents. Praising King for his work and sympathizing with the predicament of black people, Kennedy beseeched street-corner crowds to work peaceably for better conditions. Two months later in Los Angeles, after winning the California primary, Kennedy himself was dead at the hands of an assassin.

American society seemed a series of open sores. Those who opposed the course the country was taking, both at home and abroad, were faced with the question of how most effectively to make their voices heard. The question became all the more desperate as filmed coverage of the war continually poured forth from the television every evening—a constant, grim reminder that the suffering went on—and after the smoke from the April riots had cleared it was still evident that little was being done to end the social and economic oppression of black people.

Each of the "Catonsville Nine," as the group came to be known, had attempted to deal with the suffering they saw around them. Many had worked in programs of service to the poor, and all had written letters, marched, and picketed in an effort to end war and discrimination. Philip Berrigan had met with Secretary of State Rusk, trying to make known his reasons for opposing the war and questioning Rusk on the government's actions. The interview ended with Berrigan feeling that little had been gained, as Rusk had said nothing new and had given no hope that there might be any kind of reversal in U.S. policy.

The question "What can be done?" weighed heavily on them, and a feeling of helpless guilt arose as every protest was rebuffed. And yet, for the Catonsville Nine, to remain silent about the suffering they saw amounted to the same thing as a vote in favor of its continuing. At their trial a year later, Marjorie Melville, a member of the group and a former sister in the Maryknoll order, said: ". . . there comes a moment when you decide that some things should not be. Then you have to try to act to stop those things." They would, in a very real sense, lay their lives on the line and try to stop at least a small part of the system that to them was the source of the suffering.

The demonstrators were still standing around the now smoldering fire when the police arrived. One by one, the police questioned them. David Darst, the youngest member of the group and a Christian Brother, was asked if he had participated in seizing and burning the draft records. "Yes," he answered, "I wanted to say 'yes' to the possibility of a human future."

The group was arrested and driven to a jail on the outskirts of Baltimore. There they were charged with destruc-

9

tion of government property and conspiracy. These being federal offenses, FBI agents were summoned. Daniel Berrigan later wrote: "I remember the expressions on the faces of the FBI men as they entered and saw us clerics under arrest. . . . How their jaws dropped! One of them turned in disgust to a companion and exclaimed, 'I'm going to change my religion.'"

Newspapers across the country featured the story of the episode at Catonsville the next day. Accompanying many of the stories was a photograph of Daniel and Philip Berrigan, their clerical collars plainly visible, throwing matches onto the already flaming papers. To many readers, already exasperated by accounts of ghetto rebellions and campus disruptions, it was one more example of the breakdown of the structure of society. But the fact that the participants were all Catholics and two were priests was puzzling, and the group's statement—that they were attempting to act along the guidelines of their Catholic faith—was more puzzling still.

In 1968 there were over forty million Catholics in the United States. They were generally considered a more conservative element of the population. The late Francis Cardinal Spellman, the archbishop of the diocese of New York and the leader of the American Catholic establishment, had been one of the most outspoken advocates of the American role in Vietnam. On a trip to the battlefields there he had blessed American soldiers as they were going into combat and called theirs the righteous work of God. Many other prominent Catholics in business, unions, and civic organizations had identified themselves as supporters of the war effort. Indeed, among liberal intellectuals the stereotype of the average supporter of the war was a flag-waving, working-class Catholic. Against this background of ardent and patriotic conservatism the Berrigan brothers and their fellow Catholic activists burst like a bombshell.

In the months that followed Catonsville, similar actions took place around the country. In Milwaukee, Washington, Chicago, New York, and Providence, as well as smaller cities and towns, draft files were destroyed by opponents of the war. Often the participants in the raids were Catholics. People began to speak of a "new Catholic Left" that was moving to the forefront of the antiwar movement. It was in Daniel and Philip Berrigan, through their public demonstrations, speeches, and writings, that the new movement found a focus.

Philip Berrigan stressed later that the raids were not merely a tactic to disrupt the drafting of young men, but an attempt to force a changing of values on the public: to make people question the value of preserving the established law and order in the face of so much discrimination, war, and suffering. Those who participated in the draft board raids were calling on Christians to deal with the teaching of the Gospel that one must "speak truth to power" even if in speaking that truth one breaks the law.

The Berrigan brothers were the first American priests to go to jail for political reasons. Though their supporters referred to them as "political prisoners," they preferred to call themselves "prisoners of conscience," unable, according to their beliefs, to do other than they did. All their years as members of their religious orders have been marked by their prodding, pushing, and sometimes, in the eyes of their superiors, outright rebellion. But they have permanently altered an aspect of American Catholicism and have made their disturbing presence known in every corner of society. To the late J. Edgar Hoover they were "extremists" and "anarchists" who plotted violent sabotage against America. A Catholic construction worker in New York said recently: "To me, as a Catholic, they are personally embarrassing. They should be defrocked." But a young Jesuit at Woodstock College said: "They show us what we ought to be."

When asked about how they came to be such "trouble-makers," they are apt to joke about their Irish heritage. But their vision of what one must be and do to be truly a Christian in the modern era, a vision that has rocked both Church and government, is the result of all their experiences on the road to Catonsville. The story of Daniel and Philip Berrigan leads to one of the great ironies of the decade, and perhaps of the century: how it came to pass, in the late sixties, that two men who have devoted their lives to the work of God found that the only road left open to them, in this predominantly Christian country, was to go to jail in order to better serve their faith.

2

Northeastern Minnesota was still practically pioneer country in the early 1920s. It was a country of mostly Scandinavian settlers—Swedes, Finns, and Norwegians—held to the subsistence level, never quite having enough. In territory known for its harsh and cruel winters, keeping alive and warm was a constant struggle. Daniel and Philip Berrigan were the youngest of six brothers born into an Irish-German family in the small town of Virginia, Minnesota, just fifty miles from the Canadian border. Their father, Tom Berrigan, was of the first generation of Irish-Americans, whose parents came to America in the great wave of emigration following the Potato Famine that gripped Ireland through the middle of the nineteenth century.

A big man who loved both poetry and hard work, Tom Berrigan left college after two years to work on the railroad. Although it would have been possible for him to finish his schooling and pursue a business that would have supported him comfortably, as many of his relatives were already doing, Tom was passionately interested in the union struggles that were sweeping America at the time. He spent over ten years on the railroad lines, working his way back and forth across the Northeast, organizing workers for the union. His fiery spirit and his ease in making speeches made him a leader of his fellow workers. And although his family had been Catholic for generations, Tom found it difficult to bridge the gap between his religion and the union movement. The Catholic Church, always lukewarm or antagonistic toward unionism, called on its membership to stay clear of union activities. Rather than break his involvement with working-class struggles, Tom drifted away from the Church.

On a trip through Minnesota when he was thirty-three, Tom met and fell in love with Frieda Fromhart, a German immigrant whose quiet gentleness contrasted sharply with Tom's boisterous ways. They were married and settled in the Minnesota iron range. Frieda gave birth to six boys in fairly rapid succession, and beyond her chores of keeping house for her ever-increasing brood, she managed through her devoutness to bring Tom back to the Church. He embraced the faith again happily, for his disenchantment had been limited to the Church's political outlook, not its religious foundations.

The start of the Depression coincided with Tom's loss of his job as a result of his membership in the then militant Socialist party. Packing up their belongings, Tom moved his family to Syracuse, New York, where he had grown up. There was work to be found at the new electrical plants being built beside Lake Onondaga, and Tom purchased a house atop a hill overlooking ten acres of farmland. Working by day at the electrical plant, Tom enlisted the help of his six growing sons in farming the already overworked land.

The work was hard and Tom demanded total obedience from his children. Often he was harsh and tyrannical when he felt his orders were being challenged. The three older boys would at times fight back against his iron will, and occasionally Tom Berrigan would appear in the morning with the cuts and bruises of battle showing on his face. "Your brother and me had a good fight last night," he would explain to young Philip and Daniel. Being such a rebel himself, Tom no doubt felt a certain pride when his sons spoke up to him, although he would never relinquish his role as father and master.

It wasn't only farm and house chores that he demanded from his sons. Occasionally he would herd the boys into a corner and order them to sit still and listen. Then, in a booming voice that demanded to be heard, he would begin reciting poetry: Shakespeare, Yeats, and the Romantic poets would come tumbling out, repeated word for word from a memory that held several volumes of English verse.

The small school that Daniel and Philip attended offered little in the way of education. A strict and authoritarian parochial school staffed by nuns, it was a two-mile hike each way for the Berrigan boys. But whatever was lacking at school was made up by constant reading. Frieda Berrigan was forever lugging home from the library stacks of books that were immediately devoured by her six sons. At her urging, Daniel and Philip immersed themselves in *Lives of the Saints* and the Old and New Testaments. Years later, when asked to account for his rebelliousness and lawbreaking, Daniel was fond of saying he had to "plead guilty of reading the New Testament."

It was in those years that their outlook began to take shape, molded by their mother's piety and the constant activity of Tom Berrigan on behalf of all the struggling movements of his time. The first Electrical Workers' Union and the Catholic Interracial Council, which was a revolutionary development for its time, were founded in Syracuse by Tom Berrigan and other organizers. The goals and ideals that he worked toward were not lost on Daniel and Philip.

But the long shadow of the Depression fell as darkly over the Berrigan household as it did over the rest of the country. It was a time of bank closings and unemployment. While millionaires threw themselves from high windows because they had lost fortunes, workers and their families went hungry as their jobs disappeared. Farmers lost their land and homes as banks and loan companies foreclosed on their mortgages.

It was a time of loss for all, but struck worst by the Depression were those who were already near rock bottom. Millions of people took to the road, searching for work or a handout wherever it was to be found. For Philip and Daniel it was a time of hungry-looking men appearing like shadows in the kitchen doorway, asking for a bite to eat or a chance to do some chores in exchange for supper. Frieda and Tom Berrigan refused to forget their religious and social beliefs, even though there was seldom enough to feed their own large family. Whatever little they had they shared. Neighbors would direct hungry strangers to the Berrigan house as their "open-door" policy became known. The Berrigan children learned to share, unquestioningly, with those who appeared at the dinner table. There was a Spartan, equalitarian, early Christian–like atmosphere that pervaded the household all through the Depression years. For Daniel and Philip, it was the first major lesson in putting the words of the Gospel into action. They were never to forget the people they squeezed closer for at the table, who through no fault of their own found themselves with nothing except the charity of others to fall back upon.

The differences in the two brothers were already apparent. Daniel, just two years older than Philip, was a sensitive and very studious boy. Thinner and weaker than his brothers, he stayed closer to his mother. "Daniel," she said of him, "was from the age of six obsessed with the suffering in the world." He spent whatever time he could reading the books that his mother brought home from the library and the magazines that his father received. *Commonweal*, a liberal intellectual Catholic journal, and the *Catholic Worker*, the newspaper published by a small group of radical Catholics in New York living in the poverty advocated by Saint Francis and giving food, clothing, and shelter to the city's homeless, were Daniel's only links with the Catholic world outside his own parish. Their articles on the role of Christians in a troubled world jibed with Daniel's already emerging feelings of compassion toward those without.

He had inherited his father's love of poetry, and he was given to spending long hours reading and composing his own poems. It was a passion that was to grow and eventually bring him renown long before his public stands on war. His ankles were weak and special shoes had to be ordered for him. As a result he didn't care much for sports and was excused by his father from the harder farm chores. He enjoyed dreaming underneath the shade trees that surrounded the small brick house, while his brothers engaged each other in baseball and soccer.

Philip, who was tall and strong for his age, loved sports above all else. At school he was the star of the baseball team in the spring and the basketball team in the winter. Whenever there was a chance to prove himself at some physical feat he would appear and usually outdo all other comers. But his vitality at sports carried over into his reading and studying. It was Philip who, reading the news of the already approaching confrontation in Europe, would storm outloud against the injustice of the world's conditions. Closest to each other in age, and joined by their mutual desires to study and understand the confusing world about them, Daniel and Philip developed a special bond of friendship—a bond that was to grow stronger as they emerged from childhood. But first their roads were to part for a time.

When Daniel graduated from high school in 1939, he made the decision that had been forming since he had first read the heavy book on his father's shelf describing the lives of the early priests in America. He would follow his concern for others into a life of complete devotion to the teachings of Christ—a life that demanded he neither marry nor have any chief concerns outside the work of the Church. He wrote to each of the Catholic religious orders in the United States, expressing his interest and requesting information. When the replies began arriving, he was quick to note that while all the other orders seemed to be luring the prospective applicant with photographs of swimming pools and other evidence of the good life that was to be had there, only the Jesuits seemed uninterested in him. They sent Daniel a stark pamphlet containing a few quotes from Saint Ignatius, their founder—nothing more. He applied immediately. "It was an act of faith," Daniel recalled later, "on both their part and mine. I suspected they were revolutionary. I haven't been disappointed." The Jesuits accepted him and at the age of eighteen Daniel left home for the Jesuit seminary near Poughkeepsie. He was not to return for seven years.

For a young man of eighteen to decide how he will spend his entire life is an enormous step. Entering the Jesuit training center for the first time was, for Daniel, like entering a different world. But it was a world built about the ideals that Daniel held, and in the quiet, intense atmosphere of the seminary he found a very deep sense of God. The life of the novices was one of simple hard work and training. There were chores and labors to be done as well as the classroom and study work. The meals were bland and meager, portions just large enough to stimulate an appetite, never to satisfy one. The rigorous discipline exacted from the novices left little room for anything besides their work. But it was in this new life that Daniel found something he had been searching for—a sense of human community, of people living and working together toward a common and hopeful goal.

The Society of Jesus is one of the oldest and largest of the Catholic orders, and since its inception it has been controversial. Founded in 1534 by Ignatius Loyola, the Jesuits took it upon themselves to carry the word of the Church into the most remote areas of the globe. Within a few decades of the order's founding, there were Jesuits stationed on four continents, from Japan to the New World. It was their primary mission to convert the heathen, and often their duties led them into dangerous and previously unexplored areas. In America it was a Jesuit, Father Jacques Marquette, who was the first European to explore the Mississippi River. And there were many Jesuits who died as martyrs—in Japan, England, and North America—trying to spread Christianity.

Because the missionaries usually arrived in foreign countries with European colonists and merchants not far behind them, their work was often seen as an attempt at softening the native population for European expansion and exploitation. This was true in some cases, but not most of them. For instance, in Peru, Father Luís de Valdiva and his small group of Jesuit missionaries championed the cause of the Indians against white settlers who had annexed their land and attempted to enslave vast numbers of them. Appointed the administrator of Chile by King Philip III of Spain, Valdiva freed over ten thousand slaves, to the intense anger of the colonists.

Continuing into the twentieth century, the spirit of rebellion within the Jesuit order always placed it in the center of Church disputes. Their tradition of selflessness and service has given the Jesuits a reputation the world over as the most industrious and productive of the Christian proselytizers.

The order that Daniel Berrigan entered demanded the complete devotion of all its novices. Many of the young men who entered the seminary at the same time as Daniel dropped out, unable to relinquish their now forbidden habits and pleasures or to accept the rigorous life-style. But Daniel, still shy and somewhat withdrawn, buried himself in his studies and insisted on a discipline for himself that might equal the hardships of the poor, whose sufferings he tried to keep foremost in his mind. His family was allowed only four visits a year, and he was not permitted to go home at all during the first few years of his training, save in the event of an accident or sickness. Each time Tom and Frieda and one or two of their sons made the journey to Poughkeepsie, or to Woodstock College, in Maryland, where Daniel was later sent, they found him relaxed and happy with a glow of satisfaction in his eyes. The ideas, the people, and the surroundings seemed to agree heartily with him, and the mission that he had embarked upon already felt to him like his life's vocation.

Philip Berrigan, after graduating from high school, spent a year working in order to save money to attend college. He had lost none of his energy and combativeness and he plunged into his work as though it were a dare. Scrubbing engines in a railroad roundhouse, as hot and dirty a job as exists, he would emerge every day at dusk, blackened from head to foot. To add to his savings he played first base on a local semiprofessional ball team on the weekends and some evenings.

In the fall of 1942 he entered Saint Michael's College in Toronto, Canada. But America had entered the Second World War almost a year earlier and Philip realized that he would soon be called. At the end of his first semester he was drafted into the army. None of the pacifist principles that were to shape his later life had yet emerged in Philip and he was by his own admission "an enthusiastic participant" in the war. A friend said of those years: "You have to remember, Philip Berrigan is like Saint Paul, an exceptionally gifted warrior. Before his conversion, he could kill men more enthusiastically than most soldiers can." But if his scruples against killing had not yet been formed, he was still very much aware of the conditions of his fellow man, and the experiences of wartime made an indelible mark on him.

While undergoing training in the Deep South, Philip noticed and remembered the dire poverty in which black people lived, and the racist attitude that prevailed in the rural areas where he was stationed. Out on maneuvers on a very hot and humid day, his platoon was supposed to eat nothing except the K rations they would receive overseas. Tired and starving at the end of the day, Philip and a few companions came upon some black people who were selling whole barbecued chickens for a dollar apiece. A few of the soldiers bought chickens and sat down by the roadside and ravenously devoured them. As they were finishing, a southern white boy walked up, a huge grin on his face. "That ain't chicken you boys is eating," he said leeringly, "it's buzzard."

His basic training completed, Philip was shipped to England. He saw the devastation of the English cities that had been laid waste by German bombers. In Coventry, Bristol, Sheffield, and London, Philip encountered large portions of the cities that had been turned to rubble and where thousands of civilians had died. Serving in the field artillery in France and Germany, Philip's unit was involved in some of the worst fighting of the Allied offensive. Switching to the infantry in France, he was given a battlefield promotion to second lieutenant. He does not speak of this period in his life, but the effect on him of two years of combat can be gauged by the firm stand against war that he was to take later.

Returning to Syracuse in 1945, Philip found that his brother Jerry had followed Daniel into the seminary. Still unsure about his eventual direction, Philip entered the College of the Holy Cross, in Worcester, Massachusetts. Graduating as an English major in 1950, Philip, too, decided on the priesthood. His choice was the same as Jerry's: the Society of Saint Joseph, an order that had been founded in America a century earlier, and whose mission was to help black people.

While at Holy Cross Philip would often drive to nearby Weston where Daniel was studying theology. After three years of teaching at a Jesuit high school in Jersey City, Daniel was beginning to get his first inklings of how the Church could interact with the community. "Everything I had believed or hoped about myself, by way of being a contributory creature in the real world, began to come true," Daniel was to write of those years. Talking late into the night about the problems and questions that excited them, the two brothers pondered how they, as priests, could best work toward what they believed.

3

With not a little anxiety, Daniel Berrigan knelt before Richard Cardinal Cushing in the chapel at Weston and was ordained a priest. It was June 21, 1952. For thirteen years he had been studying and working toward this moment. Now, no longer was he to be taught. From this time on he was to be a teacher of men and a guide for all who looked toward the Catholic faith to find a way through the mazes of modern life. Yet he remained unsure and uncertain. Later, he wrote of that morning service: "I remember a kind of desolation, the cold of the floor on which I stretched like a corpse, while the invocation of the saints went over me like a tide, a death. . . . A most unfinished man! What would it mean to be a Catholic? Who would be my teacher?" He was to wait for his answers.

There was one more year to be spent at Weston, studying theology and scripture. But the academic side of the Church was beginning to wear on Daniel. The questions that had formed through the years of studying demanded answers from the living world outside the cloistered walls of college. So in July, 1953, when he was sent to France, it was for Daniel "like landing on a fresh air planet, after being locked up in a time capsule." Assigned to ministerial work and study in a small town outside Lyon, he rejoiced at finding himself on new terrain.

The people, the language, and the culture, products of a society over a thousand years in the making, intoxicated him with every encounter. He fell irretrievably in love with the country, and adopted it as a sort of spiritual home. "Something tells me I was born here," Daniel wrote during his first months abroad.

The problems of France became his problems as well, and he suffered alongside the French as they attempted to come to grips with a crisis that was shaking the nation. The French occupation of Indochina was coming to a bloody close, as native liberation armies won victory after victory climaxing in the battle of Dienbienphu and the eventual total French withdrawal. For the French people it was a rude awakening to the realities of the postwar world. The country was in turmoil when Daniel arrived, and the debate between opponents and supporters of French colonialism was feverish. Daniel had no way of knowing that Indochina, the subject of the furor, was to play such an important role in his own life.

Of much more concern to Daniel was the ongoing schism within the European Church over the still recent memory of the Second World War. The war had been over since 1945, but the horrors and the bitterness of that time were still being laid bare and debated across the continent. The role of the Catholic Church during the war was still an agonizing topic for all Catholics. Pope Pius XII had remained officially silent throughout the war years on the situation of the Jews in Germany and in Nazi-occupied countries. Was he at the time aware of the eventual destination of the millions of Jews who were deported to the east? Why had the Catholic bishops of Germany supported Hitler after his accession to power? Once Hitler was defeated and liberty restored to occupied Europe both Catholics and non-Catholics waited anxiously for the answers to these questions.

The pope, the Vatican said in reply, had been unaware of the ultimate horror that awaited the Jews and others shipped to concentration camps. But he had, through diplomatic channels, attempted to ease their plight. There had been no formal pronouncement by the Holy See condemning Hitler because it was felt in the Vatican that, for the sake of Catholics in Nazi-dominated lands, the Church had to remain neutral in the conflict. The Catholic hierarchy had, in fact, opposed Hitler in Germany, the Vatican claimed, citing as examples priests who had heroically hidden Jews in their monasteries and Catholics who had died in concentration camps. But for most people a great deal remained unanswered.

The changing social situation of postwar Europe, combined with what many regarded as a lack of leadership by the Church during the war, led to a steady decline in Church membership. This crisis carried over into the beliefs of the priests, who were left with the problem of how to restimulate the Catholic masses. But hardest for them to ponder was the question of how the Church had conducted itself through the most traumatic era of the century.

As a young priest just barely beginning an active role in the life of the Church, Daniel came face to face with this question. Years later, both Daniel and Philip were to see strong similarities between the moral situation of priests during World War II and their own situation during another war, the one in Vietnam, twenty-five years afterward. A brief look at that period, from which the Roman Catholic Church emerged scarred and changed, helps to shed some light on the witness of the Berrigan brothers.

Although the Church was initially opposed to this rise of Nazism in Germany, it had been forced to change this policy under the threats of persecution after Hitler had risen to power. In order to safeguard the Church and its followers, Pius XII signed an agreement with Hitler in 1933 ensuring that neither party would interfere in the internal affairs of the other. For the Catholic Church this meant keeping out of German politics entirely. Hitler for his part agreed to recognize the sanctity of churches and monasteries.

As soon as Hitler took office the program of the National Socialist party became official state policy and as a result the violent anti-Semitism preached by the Nazis was put into practice beginning in the early thirties. The daily roundup of Jews that went on throughout Germany toward the end of the decade and spread to all countries eventually occupied by the German army, was a fact of life known to all. But the deportations, combined with restrictive laws passed against the Jews, were only the tip of the iceberg. The end result of Nazi policies was the concentration camp. How many Catholics, both clergy and laymen, were aware that the Jews were being systematically exterminated at the camps of Dachau, Auschwitz, Treblinka, and others is still a source of debate. Certain priests who were aware of the full extent of Nazi policies managed to inform Church officials. But in keeping with its policy of noninterference, the Church did not publicly criticize the Nazis for the Jewish persecution.

But there were Catholics who, aware of the plight of the Jewish people, fearlessly spoke out. Provost Lichtenberg of Berlin offered a daily prayer for the Jews beginning the morning after the first roundup. He continued his prayer into 1941, when he was arrested by the Gestapo, the secret police. Under questioning he stated flatly that the deportation of the Jews was irreconcilable with Christian morality. He requested from his captors that he be allowed to accompany the deportees as a spiritual adviser. Instead, he was sentenced to two years' imprisonment for "abusing the right of the pulpit." On his release in 1943, he was again seized by the Gestapo and shipped to Dachau, where he died in 1945. In Germany, only Lichtenberg and a handful of other courageous priests raised their voices in protest against

Jewish suffering, but in other countries the Church hierarchy itself spoke out.

The bishops of Holland, as early as 1934, decried the rising Dutch Nazi movement and prohibited Catholics from joining. After Germany occupied Holland and the deportation of Dutch Jews began, the bishops publicly protested. In France, under the occupation, the Catholic clergy denounced the deportations. When the Germans seized four hundred French workmen and sent them to Germany as forced laborers, twenty-four priests disguised as workers sought to accompany them. Discovered, they were sent to prison from which none of them emerged alive.

Despite its silence on the Jewish question, the German Church still had considerable power when it raised its voice on other Nazi atrocities. This was proven by the widespread campaign spearheaded by Catholic bishops against the Nazi program of euthanasia: the execution of the aged, the mentally ill, and those with incurable diseases. For two years the euthanasia program was an open secret in Germany. In 1941, when it was learned that those severely wounded at the front, and the patients in Catholic rest homes, were to be added to the death list, the bishops publicly spoke out. Catholic bishops, from the pulpits of some of the most prestigious cathedrals in Germany, protested the slaughter, terming it a criminal act and a violation of Christian moral law that cast Germans in the eyes of the rest of the world as a barbaric people. The effect of the sermons was widespread. Copies of the bishops' protests were circulated at the front and throughout the country. Nazi officials worried that unless the program was ended, the loyalty of the predominantly Catholic provinces would be permanently lost. Shortly afterward, the euthanasia program was halted. The power of the German Catholic Church was still enough, even when the violent power of the Gestapo and Hitler's military achievements were at their height, to force the government to comply. Yet the bishops' enforcement of Christian moral law stopped short of aiding the Jews as well.

Allied emissaries to the Vatican made repeated attempts to persuade Pius XII of the importance of his publicly denouncing the Nazi Jewish policy. But the pope remained steadfast, repeating that any attempt by him to alleviate the suffering of the Jews would only condemn Catholics to the same fate.

As Hitler's Reich steadily crumbled under the advance of American and British troops from the west and the Russians from the east, the world began to find out the full extent of the horrors wrought by the Nazi regime. Concentration camps captured by Allied forces were filmed and photographed and pictures distributed throughout the world. Over six million Jews died in the camps, along with one to two million others whose existence had worried or displeased the Nazis. The awesome question that faced the postwar world was how such barbarism had ever come about.

To priests like Daniel Berrigan ordained during or immediately after the war, the question of the Church's role during the holocaust was one of agonizing importance. Had the Church fallen short of its Christian duty? The question went to the very root of the Christian belief that the new generation of priests had so recently embraced as their life's work: the commandment of Jesus to love one's neighbor.

When Daniel arrived at the Jesuit seminary outside Lyon, he found the young priests in a whirlwind of feverish activity and debate. The scars that the Church had suffered as a result of its wartime actions had not yet healed. The priests were taking steps to revitalize the church and make it once again into a religion that spoke to and answered the needs of the people. Many of the priests Daniel met were members of the controversial worker-priest movement. In defiance of the traditional priestly life-style, these men had cast aside their clerical tunics and gone to work in mills and on the docks. They celebrated Mass with their fellow workers during lunch breaks and generally tried to make the Church a part of the everyday working life of the community. For Catholicism it was a bold experiment that split the Church hierarchy between those who favored innovation and those who insisted that the traditional role of a priest was being debased.

Daniel observed the worker priests in action. He marveled at the strength of men living two lives at once, that of workers subjected to all the hardships of working-class life and that of priests dedicated to the spiritual needs of their fellows.

The storm over the movement was about to burst. Bishops were publicly denouncing the worker priests for wasting their long theological education by working as common laborers. Of even greater concern to the bishops, however, was the fact that the priests had seen it their duty to fight alongside the workers in strikes and disputes. The priests, who had soon learned the difference between self-imposed religious poverty and the everyday misery of working-class life, had thrown themselves into union struggles with the same determination with which they pursued the work of the Church. They grew to see the fight against low wages and poor working conditions as inherent in spreading the Christian faith. To their opponents they said: Had not Christ advocated helping the poor and needy, first and foremost? But for many French bishops, and especially for the Vatican, the line between union activities and participation in Communist movements was difficult to distinguish. In France, where the largest and most militant union was headed by the French Communist party, it was feared that the priests were unwittingly allying themselves with the Church's proclaimed enemy: Marxism.

But for the priests, the simplified Masses they conducted

at their places of work and the rigor of their new lives placed them on the same plane as their congregation. No longer did they have a distant and privileged relationship to the masses of Catholics. They felt strongly that they had arrived at a means of doing God's work much closer to Christ's vision than the traditional style they had left behind them. And if they now found themselves marching alongside Communists, it was because the Communists were doing many things they thought the Church ought to be doing.

In long discussions with worker priests, Daniel found a whole new world opening to him. In the struggling worker-priest movement he saw how the moral convictions that had formed his decision to become a priest could and must be part of a living Catholic faith. But a warning of the impending doom of the worker priests came early in 1954 when the pope warned against "the spirit of innovation." Soon after, an official communiqué from the Holy See in Rome ordered each priest to leave his working place and report to his bishop. Those who failed, it was noted, would be living in a grave state of disobedience. For the next month, the eyes of the nation were riveted on the several hundred priests concerned. Some priests chose to remain in the working class; the majority, however, decided against severing their marriage to the Church and returned to traditional parochial work. Within a year they were scattered in small parishes across France. To Daniel Berrigan it was a crushing blow. For a moment, it seemed to him, he had been able to see the future. Then the door was slammed shut again.

The last few months of Daniel's year in Europe were spent in West Germany, where he served as an auxiliary chaplain at a U.S. Army base. He remembers the period with some embarrassment. He worked "thoughtlessly and with a naive acceptance that had nothing to do with the cruel realities of that land and that time." But he enjoyed his contacts with the GIs, whom he found "unusual and delightful fellows." It was the military chaplains at the base who most impressed him. Tireless workers, who, Daniel felt, exerted a strong influence on the young soldiers, they remained military men to the core. Yet despite their hard and steady work on behalf of the soldiers, Daniel felt they did not raise the questions at the heart of the Gospel—questions that for Daniel had come into sharp focus over the past few months.

The period spent on the vast overseas military reservations of the United States was a fitting end to Daniel's year in Europe. His expectation at the start of his sojourn was that somehow he would come to grips in real life with the problems and questions that had arisen out of his years of study. The expectation was more than met in the brief but eye-opening and heartrending encounter with the worker-priest movement. And if the worker priests gave him a glimpse of what the future might be like, the recent past of the Church in Europe gave him a clue to the future of a religion estranged from the sufferings of the people. The Army chaplains were a reminder of the work that remained to be done.

Leaving Europe in the summer of 1954, Daniel looked forward to his return to America. Everything he had learned in Europe, he carried home with him like an arsenal of guns. It was his intention to fire them off at his first opportunity, in the halls of American orthodoxy.

4

The national scene that greeted Daniel on his return seemed
to hold more despair, but also more hope, than he had anticipated. The cause for despair was the same fear that
hovered over all Americans during that time. The "Red
scare" was still the number-one topic in the news, with daily
allegations of "Communist sympathizers" in high places
crowding each other on the front pages. The actions of Senator Joseph McCarthy and his committee, as well of those of
other investigative bodies, created a climate of fear and
suspicion. As a result, anything that could possibly be labeled progressive was viewed by millions as "Communist
tainted." Teachers, politicians, and even the clergy steered
clear of topics and programs that might cause the finger of
suspicion to point in their direction. Some of the most
vehement supporters of Senator McCarthy and his attempts
to expose "subversion" were prominent Catholics, with
Cardinal Spellman and the Catholic War Veterans at their
head.

But the national climate was the sort of challenge that
Daniel welcomed, and with his appointment as a teacher of
French and theology at the Jesuit-run Brooklyn Preparatory
School he was given the chance to convert some of his ideas
on Church activism into reality. He became priest in charge
of the local chapter of the Young Christian Workers, one of
the few Catholic organizations with a reputation for progressive action. He engaged the group in community work

among the blacks and Puerto Ricans of East Harlem. He also introduced the group to another side of Catholic activity: the Catholic Worker movement on the Lower East Side of Manhattan, which was involved in aid to the unemployed and work in settlement houses. For Daniel as well as the students it was an invigorating change from the classroom ideals of the Church to the realities of the New York streets.

The three years that Daniel spent in Brooklyn were a period jammed with experimentation. If ending poverty was his first concern, his second was the relationship of laymen and clergy. In addition to his teaching and his YCW work, he took on the directorship of his parish's Walter Ferrell Guild, an organization aimed at increasing the participation of laymen in the Church. It was unmapped territory for the most part, the roles of the clergy and laymen having remained separate for most of the Church's history. But within a short time Daniel had the Ferrell Guild meeting in the church basement, sipping cocktails and discussing modern literature. It was a joint effort of the priest and the laymen: Daniel sought to learn as much from them as he taught. There were many who felt Daniel was doing more to lessen the barriers between the two strata of the Church than any other Catholic in the country. The more traditional members of the parish were disturbed at the new form of priesthood that Daniel offered them, at his almost impish grin and his insistence on first names for everyone. This was not the model of a priest. But among liberal laymen and many young seminarians, Daniel's work with the Ferrell Guild and his YCW chapter brought him a reputation around New York as a forward-looking priest with something different to offer.

In 1957, Daniel was appointed a professor of religion at Le Moyne College in Syracuse, New York. Happy to be near his parents again, he continued and expanded the kind of activist priest role he'd been evolving. His brother Jerry, who had left the seminary only a year before ordination, was living in Syracuse now as well, and with Jerry's wife, Carol, they began various projects in the community. The same year Daniel's first book of poems, *Time Without Number*, was awarded the Lamont Prize for poetry. Nominated for a National Book Award as well, the book went through three printings, a remarkable feat for poetry. Publishers clamored for more from the poet-priest, and he found himself in a position where practically anything he wrote automatically found a publisher. For a man who enjoyed putting many of his thoughts down on paper, it was a helpful outlet and one that he was to make constant use of.

Corresponding with Philip, who, two years out of the seminary, was teaching at a Josephite high school in New Orleans, Daniel shared with him his experiences in Brooklyn and Syracuse and his plans for future work. Both brothers were getting a taste of the frustrations and rewards of priests who demanded more from the Church than it often wanted to give. And both were stiffening their resolve to push the Church and the laity before them, step by hesitant step.

Philip's high school was deep in the New Orleans ghetto. His massive frame and deep gravelly voice impressed his students. But he was a white teacher in front of an all-black class and he struggled to overcome the natural barriers between them. He found much of the time-worn Josephite approach to its work patronizing and condescending toward black people. Among some of his fellow teachers there seemed to be an ingrained attitude that "we enlightened whites must help these unfortunate blacks." Above all else, Philip strove to eliminate this attitude from his relationship to his students as well as to the people in the community. From his earliest encounters with black people, Philip had come to respect and admire them with a reverence he held for few of his white contemporaries.

35

From the moment of his arrival Philip had plunged into the civil rights movement that was beginning to shake the foundations of the Deep South. In Montgomery, Alabama, Martin Luther King, Jr., a young black minister, had led a successful fight to end discrimination on the city's buses. Within a year similar battles were being fought in virtually every state in the South. Philip and other Josephite priests went to work in voter registration drives, attempting to register the vast numbers of black citizens who, through fear or ignorance, had never utilized their right to vote. Philip found the atmosphere as inescapably racist as it had been during boot camp years before. Black people still suffered second-class citizenship and were even subject to violence if they protested. Philip felt it would take nothing short of revolution to change these conditions. He tried to persuade his Josephite superiors to engage the order more deeply in the civil rights struggles that were springing up all about them, but, despite the fact that the Josephites were totally devoted to the well-being of black people in America, Philip found them reluctant to go beyond the means of aid, instruction, and charity they had evolved over a hundred years of practice. Teaching the children and guiding black Catholics was the extent of their mission.

When Philip recruited groups of students to participate in picketing segregated restaurants, he was rebuked by his superiors. His other work, though, he managed to continue unobstructed. The Catholic Church in many southern towns revealed almost a split personality. On the one hand the Church had, through various declarations and communiqués (not to mention the message of the Gospel itself), confirmed the equality of all races in the eyes of the Lord. Yet, on the other hand, most white Catholics maintained the bigoted notion of white supremacy, a view reflected in separate churches for blacks. In New Orleans, Philip became instrumental in starting the first communication between white parishes and black ones. It was an optimistic attempt to attack racism at its root by undercutting fear and hatred before they flamed into violence.

Philip sent graduates of his school north as scholarship students at Le Moyne while Daniel, as excited as Philip about the new developments in the South, recruited Le Moyne students for work in the civil rights movement.

Daniel's efforts at stimulating the college and the community into a greater awareness of the problems of society were having their effect. Along with Jerry and Carol, he created a minor stir by picketing the Niagara-Mohawk electrical plant in protest against discriminatory hiring practices. In his conversations with teachers and friends, he urged them to live in Christian poverty, in the ghetto, without cars or comfortable homes. His soft-spoken, serious, but charming manner made many of Syracuse's liberals feel ill at ease, for he insisted that they practice what they preached—something few were prepared to do.

His students at Le Moyne knew him as a demanding teacher. The assignments he gave required precise answers. But his reputation as a hard taskmaster did not dissuade the hundreds of students who jostled one another to get into his classes. His lectures were considered the most interesting and dynamic on campus. He had a way of relating the most obscure theological ideas to the problems of modern life and Christianity, so that he could liven up even the dullest topic. Many of the themes the slight and smiling priest used for his lectures were considered too hot to handle by the rest of the faculty. But his crowded classrooms were evidence that the students wanted very much to listen, and to learn.

In his last years at Le Moyne, Daniel set up a house off campus for students who wanted to devote themselves fully to activism. It was a place where teachers and students were able to talk more freely and get to know each other in a nonacademic environment. It became a hatching ground for all the projects Daniel and his young crew conceived to attack the problems of the Syracuse ghetto. There, before an altar constructed by Tom Berrigan, Daniel shocked the orthodox priests by conducting Masses in English and turning the altar around so that it faced the congregation. Changes that were to become common to Catholic services around the world in a few years were still unheard of at the beginning of the sixties when Daniel experimented with them. But it was the actions of the student groups Daniel led into the ghetto that most seriously strained his relations with the Jesuit rectors of the college. Rent strikes and picket lines organized by the students and ghetto residents were often aimed at some of the main benefactors of Le Moyne, and the public's association of the school with these activities jeopardized several large contributions.

His comradely way with the students, innovations with the Mass, and ghetto activities disturbed many of Daniel's older Jesuit fellows. In 1963, they suggested he request a year's sabbatical. This considerably irritated Daniel, and some of his friends feared he would break with the Jesuits.

It was, in fact, Daniel's first crisis with his order. His disappointment deepened when, after receiving an invitation from Philip to accompany him on a freedom ride through the South, his superiors denied him permission to go. Some advice from an older Jesuit, a liberal often out of favor with his superiors, helped Daniel make the decision to remain. Thomas Merton, a well-known poet and writer with whom Daniel had been in correspondence for some time, wrote that should he quit the order, "you must consider that you are turning adrift all those who have begun to follow you and profit by your leadership, and you are also, at the same time, wreaking havoc in the minds of superiors who were perhaps timidly beginning to go along with you." Merton advised Daniel to take the sabbatical and to spend the year in Europe reinvestigating Catholic opinion there.

In the summer of 1963, Daniel arrived in Paris, still his spiritual home. But after several months, having found work and a place to live, he became dissatisfied with Parisian life. He had come to Paris in search of something, and among the prosperous, materialistic Parisians he could find little in the way of spiritual guidance. He had come expecting to meet people like the lean, idealistic priests he had known a decade before, but the worker-priest movement, with the exception of a few hardy survivors, was a thing of the past, and France, following the end of the Algerian war, was enjoying an era of peace and prosperity.

It became apparent to him that if anything was to come out of his year abroad he would have to journey elsewhere. He celebrated Christmas in Czechoslovakia, and went from there to Hungary. The sight of Catholics, often persecuted in the Russian satellite countries, maintaining their faith, did much to reconfirm his belief in the strength of the Church. The net effect of the trip on Daniel was almost a transformation. From Central Europe he went to the Vatican where he attempted to persuade the foreign office that the Church had a more practical interest in the situation of Christians in Communist Europe. Daniel asked to be sent as a Vatican delegate to the Christian Peace Conference that was to be held in Prague that summer. The Vatican was pleased with his report, but uninterested in the conference, thinking it would turn into a platform for Marxists to rail against the Western powers.

It was Daniel's first dealing with the official Vatican and he was dejected by their cynicism. He spent a few days in Rome trying to decide where to go next. He was traveling with two liberal Catholic friends from New York and they decided to take a tour of the old city. Riding a crowded trolley through the streets of Rome, Daniel noticed how all the riders weathered the jerky trip in dour silence. "The least we can do, as an international gesture of goodwill," he suggested to his companions, "is to give the passengers a little music." Then, without hesitating, he broke into Bob Dylan's "Blowing in the Wind," singing in a loud, cheerful voice. His friends joined in, and as the trolley inched along through the heavy Roman traffic, it echoed with the song as the astonished Romans looked on.

The last few days of his stay in Rome raised his spirits and he opted to attend the Prague conference as an observer without official credentials. He was the first Catholic priest ever to attend the conference, which was made up of Christians from the world over. From Africa, Asia, and the Near East, as well as all the Communist nations, Christians gathered to discuss political and social issues. What he heard gave Daniel a picture of the role that Christian churches might take in questions of war and peace, matters that governments usually reserved to themselves. Many of the participants voiced to Daniel their objections to the war in Vietnam. To Daniel it felt as though the full weight of Christian moral outrage the world over was settling on the United States for its role in Vietnam. The question of the war, which to Daniel and other Americans seemed a small and distant problem at that time, now began to take on great significance.

From Prague Daniel accompanied other American theologians to the Soviet Union, at the invitation of several Russian Christian churches. The effect, he said, was "ineradicable." With his own eyes, he saw the "other" system, which had been labeled by his own Church and government as repressive. He was moved by the small religious communities that not only managed to maintain themselves but even to thrive under a government ideologically opposed to them. And he saw Russia as a country not so different from his own. The problems of Christianity seemed equally difficult in both societies.

One other brief trip served as an eye-opening experience. The Easter preceding the Prague conference Daniel journeyed to South Africa at the request of an archbishop there. The two weeks of intense exposure to the rigidly segregated, police-like state was for Daniel a frightening experience. He met many white South Africans who, though opposed to their government's apartheid system, which subjected blacks to harsh restrictions on their social and economic dealings while the whites enjoyed a privileged role, did not know how to conduct a struggle against it, or were hesitant to do so. "I remember the question being raised, 'What happens to our children if things in the fight against apartheid go so badly that we have to go to jail?' I remember saying I could not answer that question, not being a citizen of that country, but I could perhaps help by reversing the question. What happens to our children if we do *not* go to jail?"

Daniel's answer may have surprised even himself. His travels through Europe, Africa, and Russia had led him to realize "what it might cost to be a Christian. What it might cost even at home, if things continued in the direction I felt events were taking."

From the Catholics in Eastern Europe he had brought a message, a way for Christians to live. He saw their small and threatened congregations as "communities of risk" not unlike those of early Christians. Though they lived in poverty and persecution, they still pursued their Christian beliefs. Daniel envisioned a Christianity in the West purified by persecution, refusing to fall into line with the demands of the state, always owing a higher allegiance to its religious values. ". . . What a great feeling," Daniel wrote of his experience behind the Iron Curtain, "to be in a country where there is no head of state going to Church every Sunday and corrupting it."

In the autumn of 1964 Daniel left Europe for the United

States. His outlook on the Christian life had been confirmed everywhere he had turned during his travels. At the time he left America his priesthood had seemed almost a hindrance in the performance of his missions. Now it was a weapon he would use to prod Catholics and others who professed the Christian faith but saw no contradiction between following the warlike dictates of the state, and those of Christ.

America was gradually becoming increasingly involved in the Vietnam war. Philip, transferred to a Josephite seminary in Newburgh, New York, after six years of work in New Orleans, wrote Daniel that he was anxiously awaiting his return. For the two brothers now to be only an hour's drive from each other after nearly two decades of separation, the approaching year would be a time of testing and a time for action. The religious, social, and moral outlooks of Daniel and Philip Berrigan were on a collision course with the events of the mid-sixties.

5

The activists of the civil rights movement were escalating their tactics and increasing the number of targets in the early sixties. Now, no bastion of segregation or discrimination was safe from the picket line or the sit-in. Even after his transfer from the Deep South to the urban North, Philip continued his militant involvement in the struggle for equality. Working in the ghetto of Newburgh, New York, providing food, clothing, and legal services for the black residents, Philip was still ready and eager to jump into the fray when a major battle seemed to be brewing elsewhere. But his frequent jaunts around the country on freedom rides and tours of duty on the picket line often brought words of caution from his Josephite superiors and an occasional rebuke.

In 1963, a major sit-in was called by a coalition of civil rights groups at the segregated bus terminals of Jackson, Mississippi. Following the developments of the upcoming demonstration, Philip was anxious to fly to Jackson to take part. The sit-in was sure to bring many arrests and cause a commotion that would work its way into the week's headlines. No Catholic priests had been arrested as yet at any civil rights demonstration. Philip wanted the nation to see a Catholic priest in the thick of the fight—being unceremoniously hauled off to jail. It was his duty, he felt, to be in the forefront of this struggle, and the duty of all Catholics to be there as well.

But other Catholics disagreed. Philip, already an hour in

the air enroute to Mississippi, was the subject of an urgent phone conversation between the bishop of Jackson and Philip's Josephite superior. Keep Berrigan out of the Jackson sit-in, the southern bishop warned, or there would be a direct complaint filed in the Vatican against the Order of Saint Joseph for meddling in the affairs of his diocese. Changing planes in Atlanta, Philip was paged to the phone. Ordered by his superior to return immediately to New York, he obeyed. But not without letting the world know that a priest, on his way to the sit-in, had been turned back by the Catholic hierarchy. The story flashed across the teletype, and by the time Philip arrived back at New York, a crowd of newspapermen and supporters was waiting to greet him. It was the first time national attention had focused on either of the brothers. For Philip it was his first major collision with authority.

What seemed to be the imminent possibility of nuclear warfare in the late fifties and early sixties had pushed Philip to become a pacifist. Although the teachings of Jesus speak most clearly on the issue of violence, urging mankind to "turn the other cheek," pacifism is not an enforced tenet of Christianity. Philip's openly espoused pacifism isolated him even more from the old-guard Catholics. But to the new generation of priests in colleges and seminaries across the country, Philip's unorthodox outlook, combined with his fame as the Catholic firebrand of civil rights, accelerated demand for him as a lecturer. Appalled by the devastating capacity for nuclear overkill that the United States and Russia brandished at each other, Philip immersed himself in the facts and figures of the armaments race, presenting them to his lecture audiences and comparing them to the vast amount of work that remained undone to alleviate deprivation and starvation around the globe.

There was a direct relationship, Philip said, between the billions of dollars that the United States spent each year for

44

its military budget and the painful struggle by black people for equal rights. Had the federal government turned its attention and funds toward the poverty and discrimination that is an everyday reality for black people, there would be no need for the bloody and costly fight for freedom that was being waged by blacks in America. So Philip spoke in 1964. The events of the coming months were to force him to a deeper and more gloomy analysis.

In the early spring of 1965, two successive civil rights–connected murders brought the nation's attention to Selma, Alabama. Local black leaders, including the Reverend Martin Luther King, Jr., issued a call for citizens to join them in a protest march from Selma to Montgomery, the capital of Governor George Wallace's Alabama. Daniel Berrigan arrived with a group of Catholic priests and Protestant ministers from New York. The hostility in the faces of the troopers who surrounded the thousands of protesters milling about a small Bapist chapel was reminiscent of Daniel's visit to South Africa, another country where the population was pitted against itself in a fierce, and often bloody, struggle. The marchers, turned back by the police on several occasions, finally began the journey to Montgomery. They walked past black sharecroppers' shabby houses sinking into the red southern clay. Over two thousand strong, they consisted of practically every race and creed, all of whom had come to Selma to show their solidarity with the black movement in the South.

Newsmen questioned Daniel and the other priests as to why the Catholics "were getting in the act." Daniel recalls that he wasn't exactly sure, but that it seemed history was going to be made that week in Selma, and it wasn't enough to sit back and commiserate while reading the headlines. In Montgomery the demonstration was charged by mounted police and sprayed with hoses powerful enough to knock a man over. Daniel returned to New York, shaken but exulting

45

that so many had shown so much courage, and that the event had turned out to be a victory for the civil rights movement.

In Newburgh, Philip was continuing his efforts in the city's ghetto. With a small group of seminarians he set up a Catholic Worker–type storefront office that dispensed food, clothing, and legal help to the needy. Like Daniel's band in Syracuse, the Josephites that Philip led did not stop at charity. They took their protests to city hall, and, failing to get action, divided themselves into investigating teams. Their mission was to visit every house in the Newburgh ghetto to gather exact figures on all building violations. The speed and vitality of Philip's small movement, frequently treading on important toes, distressed both the Josephite superiors and the city fathers. But Philip, as a result of his lectures and writings, was now the most famous Josephite priest in the country, and his superiors had to stop short of ordering him to another post.

In January, 1965, President Johnson unleashed the U.S. Air Force over North Vietnam. The bombing was the first in what was to be a long series of military escalations. The initial impact on the American population was one of shock and surprise. During the presidential election of 1964, Johnson, faced with a vociferously right-wing opponent, Senator Barry Goldwater, had promised never to send "American boys 10,000 miles away to fight someone else's war." But for Daniel and Philip, along with a small group of shrewd observers of American foreign policy, the confrontation in Vietnam had been in the cards for many years. "I felt," Daniel was to write of this period, "(and I believe I shared this conviction with my brother) that this war would be the making or breaking of us both." Their first act of protest, a few days after the bombings began, was to sign (and they were the only priests to do so) a "Declaration of Conscience," pledging "total non co-operation" with the Vietnam war effort and support for all those who refused to fight there. A small and seemingly safe act, the signing of similar pledges, was to be the basis, a few years later, of the federal indictment of Dr. Benjamin Spock and others.

Philip traveled back and forth between Newburgh and New York to attend antiwar rallies and forums. There was an exuberance about the broad-shouldered, heavyset priest in those first months of protest, as though he had been building toward this moment all his life. Besides his teaching and ghetto organizing, he helped organize a new peace group in Newburgh—the Emergency Citizens' Group Concerned About Vietnam. The group scheduled a public discussion on the war to be held in late March. Historians and economists from neighboring universities were invited to speak. Notices announcing the event were pasted up about town and advertisements were placed in local newspapers. On the night of the discussion, in the middle of a history professor's account of the origins of the conflict, people from the crowd began shouting him down. It quickly became apparent that a fairly well-organized group was bent on disrupting the evening. The tumult grew and the event dissolved into shambles. The next day, the Newburgh *Evening News* described the gathering as a tool of Russian propaganda. The office of the rector of the Josephite college was flooded with phone calls demanding Berrigan's dismissal. Philip's superior refused to comply. But he ordered Philip to keep off the subject of Vietnam in public and to quit the peace group he had founded. Reluctantly, Philip agreed.

But the irrepressible radical chafed at these new sanctions. Months earlier, Philip had accepted an invitation to speak before the Newburgh Community Affairs Council. His topic was civil rights, an appropriate and traditional theme for a Josephite. But midway through his speech, after recounting the wrongs done to the nation's black people and warning of dire consequences if white America refused to heed the cry for equality, he injected another reason for the present situation. Could Americans truly expect that the brutal, inhuman treatment that had been afforded black people at home, he asked his audience, would not show itself in the nation's policies abroad? He suggested that the Vietnamese were another nonwhite people victimized by American racism.

A year earlier, Philip had called for a simple reallocation of federal funds earmarked for military purposes; they were to go instead into the community to solve the race problem in America. But full realization of the torment of the Vietnamese people had led him to connect the war abroad to the violence at home, and the linking of the two gave rise to an understanding of just how grave the struggle might become before the suffering ended.

It was not a popular theme when Philip announced it, nor was it a year later when another American, Martin Luther King, Jr., attempted to identify the link between Vietnam and the black struggle. He was hooted and jeered by a wide section of the press and the public, including many liberals who had long identified with King's cause.

Newburgh, a poor and decaying city for blacks and whites alike, where right-wing fanaticism flourished alongside repeated city scandals, was hardly ready for the theories of Father Berrigan. The association of black rights with Vietnam gave his local critics a chance to fire off their favorite salvos of Red-baiting. Even the more moderate sections of the Newburgh press criticized Philip for attempting to taint the "loyal and patriotic advocates of civil rights" with international communism. His foes did not stop with outcrys in the press. This time they threatened the rector with writing letters to the parents of every seminarian, informing them that their sons' English teacher was a Communist. The outcry from the right-wing townsfolk kept the rector's phone ringing day and night. At last, he could stand no more. Shortly after Philip's speech, the rector informed him he was to be transferred. The superior of the Josephite order called Philip personally to tell him that he must once again keep silent about Vietnam.

Philip's ouster from Newburgh was headlined in the liberal Catholic press. Friends and fellow priests from around the country called to commiserate with him. But for Philip, his removal was far from a defeat. If anything, the exuberant priest considered it a victory. The question of Vietnam was now out in the open and was being threshed out in Catholic journals and on campuses. And he had managed, in his distinctive way, to speak truth to power, regardless of the consequences.

In New York, Daniel was encountering difficulties of his own. Offered an editorship of a liberal Catholic magazine, *Jesuit Missions*, after his return from Europe, Daniel had welcomed the opportunity to live and work in New York City again. He had hoped that his new job would give him the time to spend at least one day each week working in the Catholic Worker mission on Christie Street, dishing out soup or helping in the free-clothing room. He wanted to become more like the worker priests he so admired. But between his writing—he was already the author of four volumes of poetry and prose—and the peace movement he was helping to build in New York, there was little time left for manual work, refreshing as it might have been.

The Catholic Peace Fellowship was founded in 1964 by Daniel, Philip, Thomas Merton, and several people from the *Catholic Worker*. It was the first Catholic antiwar organization in the country and it quickly became a major tool for needling the Catholic community on the issues of Vietnam. The impetus for the group had come from Daniel's attendance at the Prague peace conference.

For a time, Daniel's top-floor apartment at the headquarters of *Jesuit Missions* served as a meeting place. There, in a room just large enough to accommodate a bed, desk, and file cabinet, the group laid plans for public letters, rallies, and demonstrations. The room was like a kaleidoscope of the workings of Daniel's mind at the time: Photographs of Pope John XXIII nudged clippings of Castro's speeches tacked to the wall, a rosary hung from a door handle, on the floor was a clutter of magazines and newspapers ranging from heavy intellectual journals to copies of the New York *Daily News* and an issue of *Life* magazine that perpetually lay open to an aerial photograph of the U.S. Air Force's North Vietnam targets. The few shelves of books contained thin books of the poetry of Neruda, Paz, Ginsberg, and Mayakovsky interspersed with thick volumes of French philosophy and theology.

When donations began coming in, the group managed to rent a small office in lower Manhattan. Daniel, breaking at noon from his editorial work, would meet one or two members at the office. Before sorting through letters and filing reports, a Mass was said. Daniel was still interested in the varying forms of the liturgy, and the Masses said at the Catholic Peace Fellowship office were as simple and straightforward as they were radical. Bread and wine were taken out of a desk drawer, there would be a reading of a brief passage from the Bible followed by a second reading— this time taken from a poet or philosopher. A brief prayer and then the breaking of bread and sip of wine.

Somehow, word of the small and unorthodox Masses got to the Catholic chancery and, through Daniel's patient but often worried superior, Father Patrick Cotter, the message was passed on to Daniel to stop them. Arriving for the noon ritual at the CPF office, James Forest, a close friend and coworker found Daniel quiet and dejected. A silence filled the room as the two men sat facing each other. Then Daniel abruptly got up from the desk and left the room. Moments later, he returned carrying two slices of rye bread. Placing them on the desk next to the wine, Daniel resumed his chair and passed the Bible to Forest. A short selection was read and then the two lapsed into silence. For some time they sat, not speaking. After a long period of quiet, Daniel reached for the bread. "Let the Good Lord make of this what he will," Daniel said as the Eucharist was completed.

The rebukes from the Catholic hierarchy affected Daniel in a different way from Philip. He felt a physical hurt when his order condemned him for deviating from the official line. But Philip and Daniel had made a pledge to each other never to quit the priesthood. Despite their frequent confrontations with Church authority, they insisted on remaining active and vital voices within Catholicism. In the fall of 1965 two acts of public witness, committed by two young and dedicated Catholic antiwar activists, inspired, but also shook, the nation and the burgeoning peace movement.

On October 15, David Miller, a member of the Catholic Worker mission, stood atop the cab of a truck in front of the Armed Forces Induction Center in downtown Manhattan. The very picture of conservatism in a dark suit and narrow tie, hair as short and neat as any Wall Street employee, the solemn-faced Miller spoke a few quiet sentences into the mass of microphones and cameras clustered beneath him. He then removed a small white card from his breast pocket, and, producing a cigarette lighter in his other hand, set it aflame. It was the first time since the enactment of a new law making it a crime punishable by a severe jail sentence that anyone had publicly burned his draft card. The act caused a storm of controversy across the nation, and in the peace movement Miller's act was an inspiration to thousands of other young men who were eventually to follow suit.

Both Daniel and Philip publicly defended and commended the draft card burning, and went on to approve any nonviolent act of resistance to the government's war effort. Newspapers were quick to link Daniel's name with Miller's, for during Daniel's years as a teacher at Le Moyne, David Miller had been one of thousands of students who had trooped through his classes. Curiously, though Daniel and Miller had known each other well at that time when both were working in the Syracuse ghetto, they never spoke of war or Catholic attitudes toward it. Daniel denied the attempts made by the press to present Miller as his disciple, but said he was proud of any association of their names.

Less than a month later there was a different and more shattering individual protest. Roger Laporte, a student and an occasional volunteer in the Catholic Worker mission, squatted in front of the United Nations. Pouring gasoline over his body, he set himself afire. He died several days later. It was a horrifying ultimate gesture. Laporte was the first person in U.S. history to kill himself as a means of political protest, and this unfamiliar statement of protest shocked many Americans. But Laporte was emulating the Buddhist monks of Saigon who had publicly burned themselves to death in protest against their government. Daniel had met Laporte just once, and only briefly. But this time the rumors linking Daniel's name with Laporte's were more sinister. Some said Daniel had counseled the youth and led him to believe that the greatest sacrifice would be for an American to burn himself in protest. The rumors were unfair and untrue.

After Laporte's death, Daniel learned from mutual friends of theirs that Laporte had admired him from afar and that he had expressed a desire to get to know him. But the second meeting never took place. Asked by the *Catholic Worker* to give the sermon at a memorial service, Daniel accepted. "He gave his life so that others might live," Daniel told the gathering. Neither he, nor the *Catholic Worker*, considered Laporte's action a suicide. They saw his act as an attempt to force others to choose life instead of death. The refusal to repudiate the self-immolation of the young Catholic infuriated Cardinal Spellman's chancery. It was soon to lead to a showdown between the right-wing Catholic authorities in New York and the radical young Jesuit.

Cardinal Spellman, asked about his views on the American role in Vietnam, had replied with the classic patriotic remark: "My country, right or wrong." As head of the diocese of New York and the most important Catholic spokesman in America, Spellman was listened to when he spoke. But even within Spellman's own diocese, militant Catholic opposition to the war was making its voice heard. This made a confrontation inevitable. Daniel and Philip, who had become widely known as the two leading Catholic opponents of the war, were the focus of the clash. Philip, already ousted from one parish for his outspoken opinions, was in Baltimore antagonizing the diocese and worrying his superior with frequent statements of support for war resisters. Daniel, living just a few blocks away from Spellman's chancery, was a more vulnerable target.

Working feverishly, Daniel, in the days after Laporte's death, helped to organize a new antiwar group, this time an interfaith one—Clergy Concerned About Vietnam (later enlarged to include laymen). The first public meeting was to be held November 30, in a Protestant church in New York.

On November 18, Father Cotter walked into Daniel's top-floor apartment. "The fat's in the fire," he said.

"I haven't got much fat," Daniel replied, "and where's the fire?"

"You've got to take a trip."

It was, as Father Cotter explained to Daniel, the lesser of two decisions that had been debated within Spellman's chancery. He wouldn't reveal what the alternative had been, but it was evident that expelling Daniel from the priesthood had also been discussed. Cotter pleaded with Daniel to accept his sentence and not disrupt the diocese with a debate about authority.

Cotter suggested that Daniel make a tour of South America for *Jesuit Missions*, but for Daniel it amounted to exile from New York. After his superior had left, Daniel sat stunned and disappointed. New York was where the movement was being built, person by person, speech by speech. Calling his friends and coworkers, he sounded them out about how he should react. It was felt by those most closely involved in antiwar organizing that should Daniel resist the order, the debate would be limited to a question of whether Spellman's chancery had the authority to expel him from New York. The ideas that were most important—the war, and resistance to it—would be lost in the shuffle. Better to accept the exile and then let the struggle take place on the grounds of suppression of conscience by the hierarchy. It was sound advice. Arrangements were made to keep Daniel posted on all developments, and within a week he was winging south.

At the meeting of the Clergy Concerned About Vietnam an empty chair was placed between the other cochairmen, Rabbi Abraham Heschel and Reverend Richard Neuhaus. A large sign placed in front of it read: DANIEL BERRIGAN, S.J. In Daniel's stead, Philip Berrigan gave the opening speech, a devastating attack on the war.

In the chancery of Cardinal Spellman, the opponents of the Berrigans and the Catholic antiwar movement thought they could rest a little easier with the noisy and troublesome Jesuit now out of the city. But for them, it was just the calm before the storm.

6

The story of Daniel's exile spread like wildfire across the Catholic campuses and seminaries of New York. Hard on its heels was the news that two other priests, Daniel Kilfoyle and Frank Keating, had been ordered to withdraw from the Clergy Concerned About Vietnam. The long-simmering dispute between the conservative chancery and the liberal, antiwar Catholics now burst into the open. In its lead editorial the week after Daniel had been ordered out of America, the liberal Catholic magazine *Commonweal* called the ouster "a shame and a scandal, a disgustingly blind totalitarian act." The *National Catholic Reporter* also took the chancery to task for its action. The dispute made its way into the daily New York papers with the *New York Times* giving coverage of the editorials in the Catholic press and the reaction of the friends and supporters of the ousted Jesuit. But from the chancery there came only a refusal to comment on the situation. Father Cotter, when asked about the orders aimed at the activist priest, denied that Berrigan had been silenced or exiled. The trip to South America, he insisted, was a routine reporting assignment for *Jesuit Missions*.

Critics of the Catholic Church in America have often accused it of hushing up its inner controversies. The chancery repeatedly refused to comment on the charges that Berrigan had been sent into exile, and that it had ordered the other two priests to quit the antiwar group. Perhaps the

Catholic authorities imagined that silence was the best defense against the onslaught of accusations. But it took very little to convince most Catholics that Father Cotter's denial was simply untrue. Daniel had been in and out of the news ever since his return to New York a year earlier and each time it was due to another outcry against the war. It was widely known, even among those not involved in peace work, that Daniel had been one of the driving forces behind the formation of the new clerical, interfaith antiwar organization, so why should he suddenly of his own desire leave America just ten days before the first scheduled meeting of the group? If the chancery assumed that silence was the best policy, it erred gravely. Unaware of the great dissatisfaction on most Catholic campuses because of Cardinal Spellman's stand on the war, it underestimated the reaction that Daniel's ouster would cause. And the chancery was hardly prepared for the movement that was launched to bring the controversy out into the open.

On December 5, beginning just a little after noon, about fifty seminarians and students, most of them from Fordham University, assembled in front of the offices of the Archdiocese of New York. Leaders of the group walked into the chancery and requested a meeting with Church officials to discuss the suppression of the three priests. They were told there was no one available to discuss the matter. The leaders returned to the gathering on the sidewalk and in a few moments picketing of the chancery by Catholics for the first time in its history began.

Carrying signs that read: END POWER POLITICS IN THE CHURCH, EXILE AND CONSTRAINT ARE THE TOOLS OF TOTALITARIANISM, SAINT PAUL WAS A REBEL, and MERRY CHRISTMAS, DAN, WHEREVER YOU ARE, the demonstrators walked back and forth in front of the large brownstone building. A woman passerby stopped in astonishment and watched the procession. Not sure she could believe what she was seeing, she asked a reporter standing nearby, "Are they picketing the Church?"

Twice more the leaders of the demonstration asked to speak with Church officials but again were refused. At three o'clock the rally broke up. The next day a full-page ad in the *New York Times* publicly challenged the chancery to deny its action and condemned it for the suppression of debate. Sponsored by the quickly formed Committee for Daniel Berrigan, the ad was signed by a large number of prestigious names. Cardinal Spellman was in Rome attending the Vatican II Council meetings, and the chancery remained shrouded in silence. It had hoped that the protest against Berrigan's ouster would be limited to the small number of people actively involved in Catholic peace actions and had not counted on the outcry spreading as far and wide as it had.

The work of the Catholic Peace Fellowship went on despite its thinned ranks. Taking ads in the *National Catholic Reporter, Commonweal,* and *Ave Maria* (another liberal Catholic magazine), it called the war "morally unjustifiable, an objective violation of the laws of God and a betrayal of our national tradition of respect for the democratic process." It condemned the tactics of the United States as well as those of the Vietcong and all others who would use violence to reach their ends, and declared the group's solidarity with all those who refused to serve.

The gathering storm of unrest and outrage over the war was being joined daily by thousands who could no longer comprehend the policies of the U.S. government in Vietnam. On December 3, the National Council of Churches, an association of Protestant and Eastern Orthodox churches, condemned the bombing. "We believe," the council's statement read, "that if the U.S. follows a unilateral policy in Vietnam, no conceivable victory there can compensate for the distrust and hatred of the U.S. that is being generated each day throughout much of the world because we are seen as a predominantly white nation using our overwhelming military strength to kill Asians."

While the antiwar movement was gaining strength and allies, the magnitude of the Vietnam conflict continued to grow. As daily U.S. bombings of North Vietnam created severe hardships in that country, her two most powerful backers were increasing their support. The rise in Soviet and Chinese aid to North Vietnam brought demands from sections of Congress and the military that the two largest cities, Hanoi and Haiphong, be bombed, a step the govenment had hesitated to take. Nowhere on the horizon was there any evidence that the tension would lessen, and both supporters and opponents of U.S. policy were agreed that things would get much worse before they got any better. In the city of Cuernavaca, Mexico, Daniel Berrigan, evicted from his community and cut off from the work that had involved him so totally for over a year, wrote in his journal of the ever-enlarging scope of the work that needed doing: "What is the task before us? It is as large as life itself, and remains so even when times of crisis or war narrow it to the compass of a needle's eye, to a simple *no* to war and violence."

The expulsion from America and the prospect of perhaps a permanent exile was a "terrible burden, a terrible weight." "The important thing was not that injustice had happened to me," he wrote. "The important thing was that injustice had happened at all . . . the defeat of good work, the silencing of truth, this bit deep." The first weeks of exile were spent pondering his position adrift in a foreign land, his life dislocated and abruptly broken off. It was a moral and personal crisis that brought all his beliefs and faith into question. His journal of that time records the tortured struggle that went on within him to keep this greatest setback of all from breaking him.

But as a friend later recalled, sending Daniel Berrigan to

Latin America was like tossing Br'er Rabbit into the briar patch. Together with Father Alden Stevenson, a Jesuit sent south to join him as a photographer on the journey, Daniel set out to discover the conditions of his new terrain. The poverty and squalor they found in every country they visited only served to further radicalize Father Berrigan and turned Father Stevenson, a moderately liberal priest at the start of the tour, into a firm opponent of what he viewed as U.S. imperialism. They visited ten countries in four and a half months, meeting with slum dwellers, Church leaders, young American Peace Corps workers, and government officials. Everywhere they found distrust, suspicion, and often outright hatred of the United States. U.S. policy based on corporate profit, and not the well-being of its southern neighbors, had brought this about. In South America the division in the ranks of the Church was even more severe and of greater proportions than the one developing in the north. Priests and laymen were lining up on either side of the major question of the continent: What, if anything, was the Church going to do about the intolerable conditions among its people? Camilo Torres, a thirty-six-year-old Colombian priest who had been missing for several weeks since his call for armed revolution against the government and his subsequent defrocking, was shot by Colombian troops engaged in a battle with guerrillas. The news of his death reached Daniel the same day he toured a Brazilian slum where the local priest was said by the inhabitants never to be seen in the streets of the community except when there was to be a wedding, for which he charged $145 for his services. Photographing and writing about the appalling conditions they found, Daniel and Father Stevenson frequently discussed whether the situation could be remedied by anything short of the path advocated by Father Torres.

In São Paulo, Brazil, the two American Jesuits met with

59

South American worker priests. For Daniel the encounter was one of delight and joy. As he walked through their poor and barren rooms and into the simple chapel that the priests had built themselves, his faith and belief were renewed. He had almost come to believe, he recorded, "that rightist politics, rational bias, favor of the powerful and rich, that these were winning out. Or, one was sick at heart and resigned to losing, to being alone . . ." In the space of the few hours spent talking with the priests, he decided again that the Gospel was as valid as ever, that if the Church could be on the one hand a bastion of reaction and ally of oppressors, it was still capable of being a lifegiving and revolutionary force.

Shortly after their arrival in Buenos Aires there was word of an open letter sent to the bishops of Brazil from twenty-seven priests demanding that the Church confront the problems of the country with honesty and truth and not attempt to misuse the name of Christ in the service of personal interests or in support of the dictatorial regime.

From their talks with priests and Church officials it was evident to Daniel that the time when the Catholic Church in Latin America quietly acquiesced in the totalitarian rule of local governments and stood by while its congregation suffered from malnutrition, lack of education, and the other plights of poverty, was rapidly drawing to a close. Camilo Torres, the worker priests, the open letter from the twenty-seven—all these pointed toward a new age for the Church.

The arrival of Daniel and Father Stevenson in Rio de Janeiro coincided with one of the worst natural catastrophes in that city's history. A tropical storm lashed the city on the night of January 6. As Daniel described the initial onslaught of the rain, "it was like the heavens opened up." It continued for four days and four nights. Even the port city of Rio, sheltered from the Atlantic Ocean and accustomed to sudden and heavy rainstorms bursting in from the sea, was unprepared for the unrelenting torrent. On the fifth day, when the sky finally cleared, the citizens of Rio went out to inspect the damage. Father Stevenson and Daniel made their way to the outlying slums that covered the sloping hills surrounding the city. The people there, living in homes constructed of tin and cardboard, had not had a chance once the rain loosened the earth on the hilltops above them. Mudslides had begun pouring down the hills in the night, while the slum dwellers slept, and struck them without warning. People, homes, and animals were swept down the hillsides to the bottom, where, as Daniel later described it, "they fell into a stew of death." One hundred and sixty were known dead on the fifth day, when the two American priests visited the scene, and dozens, possibly hundreds more, were suspected buried beneath the mud. Trudging through the rubble with a Catholic community organizer who lived in the slums, Daniel was asked: "My friend, millions for the war in Vietnam . . . and this for us?" Years later, at the trial of the Catonsville Nine, Daniel recounted the story of the tragedy he had witnessed in Rio as an example of the experience that had led him to resistance against the government. Listening to the episode with sympathy, the judge was astounded at the slum dweller's innuendo that the U.S. government had contributed to the floods. "I think," Daniel replied, "the fact was a bit more subtle than that. I think he was saying the resources of America, which belong in justice to the poor of the world, are squandered in war, and preparation."

For Daniel, the tour of South America was full of bitter evidence that the United States was more concerned with propping up the shaky dictatorships that ruled the majority of those countries than it was in improving conditions there. Vast amounts of technical assistance and millions of dollars were sent south, but the money was used to provide the countries with powerful police forces and military might to resist armed revolution. The Peace Corps, the U.S. government's answer to poverty abroad, was limited to small projects that barely made a dent in the prevailing conditions. The young Americans Daniel and Father Stevenson encountered who were engaged in Peace Corps activities were often bitter and angry at their situations. While they worked night and day to improve sanitation in villages, irrigate fields, introduce modern farm equipment to the natives, and improve the image of the United States abroad, many of them were quick to realize that their "good deeds" could never erase the conditions created by the feudal landowning structure whereby a handful of people owned most of the land while the rest eked out a sordid existence on tiny farms. On top of this, in Venezuela, Bolivia, Ecuador, Peru, Uruguay, Paraguay, and Brazil the major resources were in the hands of American-owned companies. And while these companies provided employment for large numbers of natives, the nature of the work and the subsistence wages paid kept them in a never-ending state of poverty. The profits from the exploitation of resources were divided between the owners and the national governments, which were usually loath to distribute them in any kind of equal fashion among the populace, even for roads, schools, or hospitals. As Fathers Berrigan and Stevenson traveled through South America they steadily collected material for their *Jesuit Missions* articles, slashing indictments of U.S. policy. Daniel's eyewitness accounts of South American conditions fed the growing Catholic activist movement in the United States.

Daniel received intermittent reports during his journey of the protest being mounted on his behalf at home. In December he had written James Forest at the Catholic Peace Fellowship that he was convinced that "great things are in the wind." In February, in Chile, Daniel got a letter from the Jesuit provincial in New York. He was assured that he would be welcome back in the city, and that his future work would be unobstructed. For Daniel, it was a great relief, and he was overjoyed at the prospect of getting back to work.

The furor created by Daniel's supporters had not quietly subsided after the picketing of the chancery. Many seminarians and young priests had been radicalized as a result of Daniel's suppression and each week a new demonstration would take place on Catholic campuses around New York. Several hundred young Jesuits had declared their intention to leave the order if Daniel was not allowed to return. All in all, the adverse publicity created by the exile and the serious disruption it had brought to Catholic schools was more than the Jesuit superiors could put up with. They began negotiating with Cardinal Spellman's office to bring Daniel back to the country to end the outcry. According to sources in the chancery, Spellman had wished the exile to be permanent, but he and his aides were persuaded by the logic of the Jesuit provincial who argued that as a result of the chancery's action hundreds of potential Daniel Berrigans had been created and that the storm would know no end.

Daniel remained in South America an additional four weeks in order to finish his reporting. On March 8, he arrived in New York where he was met by hundreds of his supporters and friends. There was a party celebrating his return that evening at the offices of *Jesuit Missions*. The following day he held a news conference at the Hotel Biltmore. He announced the publication of two new books. *They Call Us Dead Men*, a collection of essays on the Church and society, and *No One Walks Waters*, a book of poems. Publicly, he thanked all those who had marched, picketed, signed advertisements, and written letters to publicize his predicament and demand his return. Daniel assured the assembled reporters, priests, and seminarians that he was not about to alter the kind of work he had been involved in before his departure. He told them: "Our presence in Southeast Asia represents a contempt for the rights of innocent individuals and constitutes a continuing divergence, for the purposes of destruction, of resources that are badly needed in other parts of the world." He could see that the peace movement had grown, he said, and that he himself would be wasting no time in rejoining it. "No limits, except good sense or good conscience, are placed on any friendship, my freedom of speech, or any writings," he said. Father Cotter, standing at his side, played the diplomat to the end. Father Berrigan had never been silenced or exiled, he maintained; he was merely returning from a successful routine assignment for *Jesuit Missions*, and Father Cotter was happy to be welcoming him back. Friends noted that Father Cotter did seem quite relieved.

That week Daniel was back at his desk in the Catholic Peace Fellowship office, writing a long memorandum to the staff concerning priests in the military, suggesting questions to be raised in articles and letters: Hadn't Pope Paul and Pope John denounced war? If the attitude of the Catholic Church was "War never again!" how could it condone sending its priests to bless troops before they went into combat? How about bringing a group of Vietnamese Catholics to speak at churches and meetings? He spent long hours with friends and coworkers catching up on the news and discussing plans for "a spring offensive against the war." By the end of March, he was in the front line of a demonstration organized by the Clergy Concerned About Vietnam. Side by side, more than sixty rabbis, ministers, priests, and nuns marched from midtown Manhattan to a synagogue, a Protestant church, and a cathedral, pausing at each one to offer silent prayers for peace. The demonstration ended at the United Nations with a short speech and a final prayer.

One result of the controversy was that Daniel's name was now inextricably linked with the cause of peace in Vietnam. He received dozens of invitations from colleges around the country to address the students on the question of the Catholic position on the war. Already, on three occasions, tens of thousands of people had rallied in Washington, D.C., to call for an immediate withdrawal from Vietnam, but official Washington had turned a deaf ear to the protests. President Johnson had publicly chided those who opposed the war as "nervous Nellies" and implied that their opposition was something less than patriotic. The government was still refraining from bombing Hanoi and Haiphong, but the number of U.S. troops in South Vietnam had increased daily with over a hundred thousand there by the fall of 1966.

In November, the National Council of Catholic Bishops issued a statement on the war. Though it stopped far short of even mild condemnation, it indicated that many Catholics firmly opposed U.S. policies. "While we cannot resolve all the issues involved in the Vietnam conflict," the bishops' statement read, "it is clearly our duty to insist that they be kept under constant moral scrutiny. No one is free to evade his personal responsibility by leaving it entirely to others to make moral judgments." This shift in attitude was largely a result of the continuing changes that were being wrought in Rome by the Second Vatican Council. Article 82 of the council read: "Men should take heed not to entrust themselves only to the efforts of others, while remaining careless about their own attitudes . . ."

To Catholic progressives the pronouncements of Pope John XXIII, and later Pope Paul VI, and the convening of the council were constant sources of hope that the Church could renew itself sufficiently to meet the demands of the modern world. In the United States the council's effect was almost revolutionary, stirring young priests into activity and putting the older and more conservative bishops on the defensive; the power and authority of right-leaning bishops like

Cardinals Krol of Philadelphia, McIntyre of Los Angeles, and Spellman of New York were being challenged for the first time.

The work of building the antiwar movement took up most of Daniel's time through the year following his return from South America. He made a brief trip to Paris where he attempted to secure a visa to North Vietnam. The idea of "getting under the bombs" was becoming important to him. The visa was not forthcoming but he did manage to meet with North Vietnamese officials and express the position of the antiwar movement in the United States. In a lengthy letter to Pedro Arrupe, the superior-general of the Jesuits, Daniel outlined his opposition to the war and suggested that Jesuits in America be encouraged to take stands against the war and against injustice in whatever form they found it. The Jesuit authorities rejected the idea but his views were considered seriously, coming as they did from the most renowned American Jesuit of his time.

In the summer of 1967, Daniel decided to reinvolve himself in direct work with the poor. At the suggestion of Sargent Shriver, who was at that time head of the Office of Economic Opportunity, Daniel went to Pueblo, Colorado, to teach in the Upward Bound program. It was with some doubt and misgivings that he began his work. As he frequently told Shriver, he believed the war against poverty could get nowhere as long as the Vietnam war continued. How could the United States help the poor at home, he asked, while it was busy bombing them abroad? The summer in Pueblo served to reinforce his doubts. Teaching a group of fourteen young Mexican-Americans from a poor section of the town, Daniel found that the poor themselves had very little say about how the funds intended for their betterment were put to use. Leadership was not drawn from the community, but from the professional poverty fighters, whose salaries effectively cut them off from those they were trying to help.

All through the summer Daniel debated with himself as to whether or not to accept an offer from Cornell University to cohead its United Religious Work program. It was the first time the position had been offered to a Catholic priest, and Daniel was anxious to involve himself with students again because of the turbulent changes taking place in colleges across the country. At the same time, the peace movement was still struggling along and in need of help wherever it could find it. But the organizations he was most involved with, the Catholic Peace Fellowship and the Clergy and Laity Concerned, were fairly well established and continually gathering members and support. In the end Daniel accepted the offer from Cornell. There was spontaneous rapport between the Jesuit priest and the antiwar students.

On October 22, Daniel joined a contingent of Cornell students and faculty at a mass demonstration in Washington, D.C., to protest the war. Over one hundred thousand people turned out in an event that left no doubt in anyone's mind that the country was strongly divided on the question of Vietnam. Thousands of white-helmeted federal marshals battled crowds of predominantly young demonstrators who marched from downtown Washington across the river to the Pentagon where army troops in combat fatigues, their M-16 rifles at the ready, ringed the planning center of the war effort. The sharp contrast between the marchers and the police and army marked the enormous differences of opinion prevailing in the country. Demonstrators thrust freshly picked flowers into the barrels of the soldiers' rifles and tried to lure them into discussion about the war. Daniel, dressed in clerical black for the occasion, joined those who refused to obey the police order to disperse. Along with hundreds of others he was arrested.

In jail, awaiting arraignment, he was given the prisoner's uniform of blue jeans and a denim work shirt, and in his diary noted it was "a clerical attire I highly recommend for the new church." It was his first time in jail, his first arrest, and he wondered how he had so long avoided such an important experience for a radical activist. On October 27, Daniel's last day in jail, Philip, just a few miles away at the Federal Customs House in downtown Baltimore, entered the Selective Service office with a small group of companions and poured blood over thousands of draft files. Philip had escalated the tactics of protest to meet the enormity of the problem. On the day Daniel left jail, Philip entered.

7

For those who knew Philip, the blood-pouring incident in Baltimore came as no surprise. Since his ouster from Newburgh the priest's outspoken opposition to the war had become louder and more forceful, and his anguish over the suffering Vietnamese was often coupled with demands that Christians put themselves on the line to bring the war to a halt.

In the fall of 1965, when Philip first arrived in his new parish, the church of Saint Peter Claver located deep in the Baltimore ghetto, he found himself isolated from the predominantly student and intellectual support he had mustered in Newburgh. He was still under the prohibition issued by his father superior, forbidding him to speak publicly about Vietnam. But he brought all the tactics and strategies he'd learned in New Orleans and Newburgh to bear on the local problems of his new congregation. A gregarious man whose self-assurance was contagious, Philip quickly won the friendship of his new parish with his broad, disarming grin, hearty laugh, and the hefty slaps on the back he dispensed freely. Few white men are accepted as easily as Philip was, and he earned the respect and praise of some of the most militant black leaders. Stokely Carmichael, the former SNCC (Student Nonviolent Coordinating Committee) leader who led the drive in the mid-sixties for "black power," said Philip was "the only white man who knows where it's at."

As usual, Philip's methods of dealing with the problems in the ghetto brought some disapproval from fellow priests and his superiors. He started block clubs in the neighborhood and charged them with petitioning landlords to fix up buildings. Where the petitions failed to get a response, picket lines were set up. He organized an action-oriented group of black youths who did weekly checks on the extent of drug addiction and alcoholism among the residents. A center for drug abuse information was started and the first chapter of Alcoholics Anonymous in the area founded. His concept of the role his order could play in black affairs was changing, though, and he was beginning to doubt whether any predominantly white group could effectively help black people. And his conviction grew daily that no real improvement in the situation of black people in America could take place as long as the war in Vietnam continued.

In early October, 1965, Pope Paul VI made an historic journey to New York to address the United Nations. The pope's speech was a fervent appeal to the assembled government representatives to forgo all thought or intent of warfare. "Peace, it is peace," the pope told the assembly, "which must guide the destinies of mankind." In the most remarkable era of human progress, the pope said, there was a greater need than ever for an appeal to the moral conscience of man. "No more war! War never again!" It was an extension of the thought of Pope John XXIII, now presented in a country deeply involved in a costly and unpopular war. Though heads of state may have applauded the pope's comments for their wisdom and humanity, the cry for peace in a wartorn world must have been dismissed as rhetoric. But to Philip Berrigan the pope's words were a mandate to renew his public denunciations of U.S. policies.

His sermons at Mass were once again peppered with facts and figures about the war. Before his congregation he emphasized the terribly racist aspects of the situation:

Because of the poor economic position of black people in America, they made up a much higher percentage of the armed forces than of the overall population. Black soldiers were suffering a much higher casualty rate than whites in Vietnam—far out of proportion to their numbers—as a result of being sent on high-risk missions by commanding officers. And there was the simple fact that the war was being waged against another nonwhite people. But Vietnam seemed a long way from Baltimore and too many parishioners had problems enough of their own—just getting enough to eat and keeping a roof over their heads—without becoming involved in a campaign against the war. Try as he might, Philip could get little response from his congregation.

Drawing from liberal whites who lived on the fringes of the ghetto, Philip went ahead and started a new antiwar group: the Baltimore Interfaith Peace Mission. Meeting in the basement of Saint Peter Claver church, the group began with peaceful marches through downtown Baltimore. Prayer vigils were held at busy shopping centers and thousands of leaflets were printed and handed out to passersby. Arrangements were made for a small delegation to meet with Maryland Senators Daniel B. Brewster and Joseph Tydings in which the group attempted to present its views. It was slow and uneventful work, the kind of thing thousands of peace activists were engaged in throughout the country. To Philip, the situation demanded a louder "No," and the other members of the Interfaith Peace Mission concurred.

On December 29, 1966, a contingent of protesters, most of them clergymen, drove to Washington, D.C., and set up picket lines in front of the suburban homes of Secretary of State Dean Rusk and Secretary of Defense Robert McNamara. The slogans of the time were considerably less radical than they were to become: Their signs demanded a bombing halt and the beginning of negotiations, which U Thant, then secretary-general of the United Nations, had recently called for. After marching up and down in the snow in front of Rusk's house, the group moved on to McNamara's home. There, they knelt in silent prayer for over an hour before returning to Baltimore. Though pleased with themselves, they had the gnawing feeling that little of real value had been accomplished. But when Philip received a call the next day from Rusk's office asking to meet and talk with a representative of the pickets, the mood turned to one of elation. At last their voices were being heard and communication established! Philip, who was chosen to represent the group, did not share in the optimism. Through his civil rights work, he had learned how meaningless such invitations could be. As Philip suspected, Rusk was gracious and respectful, but repeated all the arguments for the American presence in Vietnam that had already been aired countless times by the administration. As for the question of morality in the conflict, Rusk grinningly told Philip that he left all moral matters in the hands of the clergy. It was the sort of attitude Philip had run into repeatedly during his years as a priest: The affairs of men were supposed to be distinctly separate from their love of God. "That guy couldn't once look at me straight in the eye," Philip reported to the group. It was decided that it was again time to raise the stakes.

A few weeks later the group invaded Fort Myers, Virginia, where the chiefs of staff of the armed forces have their homes. Approximately fifty protestors showed up for the first demonstration there. Ringing the homes with their picket signs, the group marched around and around until the provost marshal of the base appeared. Philip stepped up to the man and handed him a letter the group had drafted to the chiefs of staff protesting the support by the United States of an undemocratic and totalitarian regime in South Vietnam. The sight of the assembled clerics made the provost marshal uneasy, and in halting voice he ordered the group to leave. Philip asked what would happen if they refused. The provost marshal, made even more nervous by Philip's tone, declared, "You'll be sorry." It was a thinly veiled threat of arrest, but to Philip, the vision of some fifty mostly middle-aged clergymen being arrested by military police was delightful.

The group decided to return again to Fort Myers and within a few weeks they were driving into Virginia once more to confront the chiefs of staff. An unsympathetic newsman passed on word of the impending demonstration to the military and when the protesters arrived they found a roadblock of MPs checking all the cars. Philip raced about in his car looking for an open entrance and finally found one at Arlington National Cemetery. Another carful of demonstrators did a fast swerve around the guards, and the group met on the parade grounds in front of the chiefs of staff's homes. After a brief prayer, they returned to Baltimore. Philip, encouraged by the day's events, told his companions that they had the military where they wanted them: The next time they went to Fort Myers, the military would have to arrest them all. Otherwise word would get out that government property was fair game for all antiwar protesters. Mass arrest was the kind of protest that Philip felt would shake the public's conscience.

The increasing militance of the demonstrations was narrowing the Interfaith Peace Mission down to its most devoted members. It was an accepted fact that the next protest at Fort Myers would mean arrest for all involved, but many were not prepared for that eventuality.

The third raid on the fort in June, 1967, had only twelve participants. The demonstration began as the others had, except that this time the military had had no advance warning and the group encountered no difficulty getting onto the base. Gathering about the flagpole at the center of the parade grounds, they knelt in prayer while passages of the Bible were read aloud. As Philip looked up from his kneeling position, he saw the provost marshal, the same one they had encountered on their first protest there, hurrying toward them across the field, an army intelligence officer waddling under the weight of several cameras beside him. The provost marshal singled out Philip as a target for the photographs, and Philip accommodated him with a grin. With a sweep of his arm, the provost marshal ordered the group off the base. As had been agreed before, the demonstrators refused and, instead, in nonviolent fashion, went limp and allowed themselves to be carried onto a waiting bus by the MPs. The protesters carried on a running debate with the provost marshal and the MPs as they were dragged away. What did they really think about Vietnam? What about the possibility of nuclear war? The soldiers, trying their best to be civil, responded that they didn't really know, they were just following orders. The bus drove them to a spot outside the base where their cars had been towed by Army trucks. Very politely, they shook hands with the provost marshal and the MPs, then got into their cars and drove off. But not to leave.

Within ten minutes the protesters' cars came barreling through the fort gates again, reassembled on the parade grounds, and took up their prayers where they had left off. Within moments the enraged provost marshal reappeared. Cursing Philip and the rest of the group, he had them again loaded onto the bus but driven this time to military police headquarters. Told to wait, they sat in the bus for over an hour. Inside the MP station, the provost marshal was on the phone to the Pentagon trying to find out what the generals wanted to do with the unruly bunch. The generals were reluctant to try eight clerics and four others in court. The group was eventually driven outside the camp again and let out. In the confusion the MPs failed to discover the Reverend

James Mengel, a former army chaplain of the United Church of Christ, who had hidden himself behind the back seat. All of a sudden, as the seemingly empty bus rumbled back toward the base, Mengel's head appeared out a rear window; he was singing the civil rights anthem, "We Shall Overcome," at the top of his voice. The group stared as the bus jerked to a halt. A body was heaved from the door. Philip rushed toward the minister to see if he was still alive. As he approached the sprawling figure, Mengel suddenly leaped to his feet and resumed the song.

The day had passed without serious injuries to any of the demonstrators, but they were depressed that the army had denied them a courtroom hearing. That night, in Baltimore, they met for an emergency meeting that continued into the early morning. It was decided to escalate the protest still further, this time by destroying government property in a way that would shake the national conscience—yet still be nonviolent.

There is a thin line between the destruction of property and outright violence, and the Baltimore group was aware that it was treading on dangerous ground. Some members of the Peace Mission dropped out rather than take this risk, and Philip received long letters from close associates trying to dissuade him from an act that they felt would discredit the peace movement in the eyes of the country. But for Philip, the primary issue in nonviolence was to avoid violence to people—not things. The other issue argued by the militant members of the Baltimore mission was what use they could be to the peace movement in prison. It was a difficult question to resolve. No one could prove that the movement would be furthered by the martyrdom of a small group. In the end, the answer was faith. Who could be sure, Philip argued, what the long-range effect of such a public witness might be? What was most important, he told his critics, was that one follow one's beliefs regardless of tactical considerations or consequences. Joan of Arc, Thomas More, Martin Luther, and the early American Quakers were among those who had chosen imprisonment and worse rather than compromise their beliefs. America had a rich tradition of civil disobedience, as Philip was later to note, from the Boston Tea Party to the civil rights movement. America had reached another turning point, he felt, and it was necessary to break the law in order to serve justice.

The group trimmed down to four persons: Philip; the Reverend James Mengel; Thomas Lewis, son of a wealthy manufacturer and a deeply religious Catholic; and David Eberhardt, a poet, self-acclaimed agnostic, and son of a Presbyterian minister. Long hours were spent discussing the plan of attack. The first suggestion was to burn down an abandoned Special Forces barracks at Fort Howard, Maryland, but the idea was abandoned as too risky. The destruction of draft files had an appeal for all the members of the group, as it seemed to hit the war effort at its weakest and most discriminatory link. The means of destruction were another question. Burning, which was the initial plan, had too much of a violent nature about it. At one of the meetings, a lawyer who was in favor of the action suggested pouring something on the files. The group immediately considered a variety of liquid possibilities. At the end of a long list including detergent, paint, and honey, someone suggested blood. To Philip it was the obvious choice and the rest concurred quickly. They would not be destroying the files, it was reasoned, but simply anointing them with blood, the Christian symbol of life and purification.

On a designated evening, the four members gathered for the procedure of giving their blood. A doctor who had previously volunteered for this work changed his mind at the last minute and the group was forced to rely on a Peace Mission member who had had some hospital training. All the necessary equipment was arranged on a table and the bloodletting began. James Mengel was the first to receive the needle. Blood barely trickled from the tubing into one of the bottles being used as a receptacle. The tubing was too thin and failed to provide enough suction. Five times the volunteer jabbed Mengel with the needle trying to extract more blood. On the fifth attempt Mengel fainted. Eberhardt and Lewis were fearful that deadly air bubbles might escape into their veins and wanted to call if off for the night, but Philip felt there would not be enough time to arrange things again and insisted that they continue. Laughing at his friends' qualms, Philip ordered the volunteer to stick the needle in again and again. After twelve attempts to draw blood from Philip's massive forearm the rest of the group demanded that he stop. Rushing to a nearby delicatessen, a member of the Peace Mission bought a quantity of duck's blood. The remainder of the four quarts used in the raid came from calf's liver.

Philip has always cited his brother Daniel as his main source of inspiration. The dedication to his first book, *No More Strangers*, reads: "To my brother Daniel, without whom neither this book nor my priesthood would have been possible." In the last weeks before the planned day of action, Philip wrote to Daniel explaining the course events had taken in the Baltimore peace group. It was important to Philip that Daniel understand and approve the escalation in tactics. Even though the statements of support for draft resisters that both Daniel and Philip had signed numerous times were technically illegal, Philip insisted in his letter that it was a game the government would permit them to play indefinitely. The only way left for those opposing the war was to place themselves in jeopardy, Philip argued, by staking their own lives in the struggle. He raised the example, as he had done several times since the Vietnam conflict had worsened, of the priests in Hitler's Germany who had protested government policies even at the risk of their lives.

For Daniel, who had counseled Philip and led the way in opposing the war, his brother's arguments were invincible. They were of one mind in their total opposition to the war, but Daniel was surprised and somewhat shocked at the conclusions Philip was coming to. Safely ensconced in the academic environment of an Ivy League college, Daniel felt removed from the day-to-day work Philip was conducting. There was no need to assure Philip of his support—this went without saying. But the proposed action revealed for the first time the differences in personality between them. Daniel, the poet and intellectual, saw his role in society as a constant heckler of the powerful, a gadfly to Christians who neglected the Lord's commandments. His poems and essays often touched on the mystical aspects of Catholicism, a concern also reflected in his liturgical experimentation. For Daniel, modern Christians were, in effect, once again in the arena with the lions—and quite possibly might suffer a similar fate.

Philip was left unmoved by efforts to modernize Church ritual—he paid little attention to the developments of the Second Vatican Council. His only concern had been man's relation to man, in the here and now, with Christ's life as the intermediary. He was still the brash young football player in many respects. A close friend recalled that at his first meeting with Philip, he felt he'd encountered the huge priest somewhere else before—as the galloping quarterback on the Wheaties box. It was around his strength that the Baltimore group gathered, and there were many who would have followed him anywhere. Philip, too, saw the encounter in terms of Christians and lions, but *he* wanted the Christians to behave more like the lions.

The four members of the raiding party attended the mass demonstration in front of the Pentagon on October 22, 1967, but their minds were elsewhere. They carefully avoided arrest, lest it hamper the scheme they had planned for five days thence.

On October 27, supporting members of the Baltimore Interfaith Peace Mission gathered a group of reporters to witness the action. At a few minutes before noon, Tom Lewis entered the Customs House to make sure the guard was not on duty. As the raiders had planned, most of the office workers were out to lunch. Lewis returned to the entrance of the building and stooped to tie his shoelace—the signal that the coast was clear. Philip Berrigan and David Eberhardt, bottles of blood swinging in their pockets, crossed the street to join Lewis at the door. James Mengel was close behind them, a stack of Bibles under his arm. Philip, Eberhardt, and Lewis entered the Selective Service office. Mengel posted himself at the door as a lookout.

Without hesitating, the three men approached the head clerk. Each gave a different reason for business: Philip said he was checking the file of one of his parishioners; Lewis, that he had lost his draft card; and Eberhardt, that he was reporting a change of address. It was routine business for the clerk, who promptly went to get the requested files. As soon as she left her desk, the three men moved quickly toward the file cabinets. A commotion made the clerks look up—a dozen reporters and cameramen rushing into the office. Their cameras were already aimed at the three men pulling open drawers and spilling the crimson contents of their bottles in wide arcs over the papers. The clerks began screaming, and Mable Pearson, the head clerk, rushed to slam the open drawers shut. Another clerk grabbed hold of Philip's sleeve and tugged, but to no avail. It took less than thirty seconds for the bottles to be emptied. Mengel handed out Bibles to clerks, guards, and even reporters. Though the press had been forewarned that the demonstration would be unusual, they were unprepared for this. Their mission accomplished, the raiders took seats on the narrow bench along the wall. They waited half an hour for the arrival of the FBI, who spent another thirty minutes examining the scene and collecting evidence. There was no precedent for this incident, and police, FBI, reporters, clerks, and guards were all visibly shaken.

The four offenders were taken a few short blocks away to FBI headquarters, where they were held on federal charges of destroying government property and offered release if they would sign statements promising to reappear. Eberhardt, engaged to be married, and Mengel, the father of two children, both accepted their release, but Philip and Lewis refused to sign and were taken to jail. There, they began a fast that lasted until their hearing a week later.

Jerry Berrigan, older brother of the two priests, was sitting at home in Syracuse listening to the radio when he heard the news of Philip's arrest. A man of the same massive frame as Philip, he started crying.

8

There was a fast and furious reaction to the "Catholic Guerrillas," as some called Philip and his group. The Baltimore archdiocese of the Catholic Church wasted no time in issuing a sharply critical statement on the draft file destruction. "Its real contribution to peace is questionable," the chancery spokesman said. "We believe such actions may be interpreted as disorderly, aggressive and extreme and that they are likely to alienate a great number of sincere men in the cause of a just peace." The denunciation from the Church hierarchy came as no surprise to the Baltimore Four. But what was painful to them was the lack of immediate and strong support from the Catholic antiwar movement and other sections of the Left. The *Catholic Worker*, the newspaper of the organization that had long served as a source of inspiration to both Philip and Daniel, expressed sympathy and admiration for the men who risked jail for their beliefs, but expressed grave doubts about their tactics. The purist pacifism preached by the Catholic Workers did not allow for the violence against property practiced by the Baltimore group. Following the first draft file destruction in Baltimore and after the napalming of Selective Service records at Catonsville the following May, the *Catholic Worker* quoted the golden rule to the Berrigans: "Do unto others as you would have them do unto you."

Even nonpacifist sections of the antiwar movement questioned the act. For different reasons, many people in the peace movement agreed with the criticism made by the Church hierarchy. The action was *too* extreme, they felt, and might turn people off. Though Philip was prepared for a certain amount of flak from his antiwar cohorts, the harshness of some of the criticism within his own camp was a source of anguish to him.

The months following the Baltimore raid were a time of strain. Philip had guided the Baltimore Interfaith Peace Mission into an area of protest far beyond the activities of the rest of the movement. Now, the old tactics of mass marches and teach-ins seemed useless to the small group of militants. Year after year, Philip had been patiently engaged in organizing demonstrations, public-speaking programs, meetings with congressmen. The Customs House raid was a formal break with all that. Henceforth he would declare solidarity only with those who chose to make the same commitment as he and his three companions—to put everything, future, family, and friends, on the line for peace.

He began to break with the organizations he was still formally associated with, organizations that advocated forms of protest he could no longer support. In a long letter to his friend, James Forest, now a full-time worker for the Catholic Peace Fellowship at Philip's urging, he explained some of his reasons for resigning from the group he had helped to found. "Frankly," Philip wrote, "I take the CPF seriously only because I love and respect my friends who are in it. Not because it is realistically facing Vietnam and/ or the Cold War. . . . To stop this war I would give my life tomorrow, and I can't be blamed if I have little time for those who want to run ads in the *New York Times.* . . . As Johnson continues to have his war, and that means the probability of invading North Vietnam, we will either witness from jail, or we will go ahead with social disruption, including non-violent attacks against the machinery of this war. . . . In a word I believe in revolution, and I hope to continue a non-violent contribution to it. In my view, we are not going to save this country and mankind without it. And I am centrally concerned with the Gospel view that the massive suffering of this war and American imperialism around the world will only be confronted by the people who are willing to go with suffering as the first move to justice." The ideological split between Philip and many of his friends caused pain and confusion on both sides. But Philip, now isolated from the majority of the movement, began to seek out others who were willing to share his commitment, and "go with suffering."

Two of the Baltimore Four were having second thoughts about another scheme they were considering. James Mengel and David Eberhardt worried over the plight of their families should they receive jail sentences for a second raid. To which Philip replied: "You've got another family— mankind." But Eberhardt and Mengel asked to be counted out. Tom Lewis, the fourth member, was ready and willing to proceed with plans for another action. Like Philip, the danger they had already been exposed to fueled him with a greater enthusiasm and strength of purpose than he had had before the raid. Another Roman Catholic, George Mische, an old friend of Philip's, announced his willingness to participate. Mische, thirty-two years old, was a large man with a heavy blond moustache who learned radicalism serving with the Association for International Development in Latin America. A talkative man with an ever-present smile, Mische brought a revolutionary dedication to the small group.

Through the winter of 1967, Philip and Mische traveled across the country looking for other recruits. Philip was anxious to involve more clerics in the raids, and conceived grandiose visions of dozens of Catholics hitting several draft boards simultaneously. In March, 1968, President Johnson announced his decision not to seek reelection. The furor over the Vietnam war and the strength of the antiwar movement had virtually driven him out of office. Johnson also announced the beginning of peace talks between the powers involved. In the antiwar movement the feeling of an impending peace produced an apathy among many who had been involved on the fringes. Philip and Mische increased their efforts to compensate for this lack of militancy. Philip's trial was scheduled for April 1, and the deadline was drawing nearer. Lawyers arranged for a panel of prominent scholars to appear before the judge to urge the court to set aside the trial until the war was over, pleading that as long as the Vietnam conflict continued a fair trial was impossible. The judge denied the petition and on April 1 the trial began. As Philip and the other defendants had expected, they were convicted. The date for sentencing was set for May 27.

In the days after the conviction of the Baltimore Four the labors of Philip's and Mische's nationwide tour began bearing fruit. The first members to sign up were Thomas and Marjorie Melville, former missionaries of the Maryknoll order who had been expelled from Guatemala for assisting armed peasant groups. After their expulsion they had both quit the order and married. Guatemala had been a harsh school for the Melvilles, and when they returned to America they brought with them a determination to become active in resistance against American policies abroad. The suggestion by Philip of a carefully planned raid on a local draft board was hand-tailored to their sympathies. They brought to the group another veteran of the Maryknoll mission in Guatemala, John Hogan, who had suffered the same fate at the hands of his order because of his aid to the guerrillas. With the addition of Mary Moylan, a Baltimore nurse and a devout Catholic who had joined Philip on numerous civil rights campaigns, and David Darst, a Christian Brother from Saint Louis who had written Philip after the October raid expressing admiration, the group began to take shape.

Philip had assembled a remarkable collection of activists, all of whom had tested their mettle in previous encounters with establishment injustice and were unafraid of the inevitable prison terms awaiting them after their action. Although Philip had approached many Jews and Protestants to join the raiding group, all the members were Catholics. As Philip had discovered, there was a great upsurge among many Catholics who wanted to break with the silent complicity their Church had shown throughout the upheavals of the sixties, while Jews and Protestants had been in the forefront of the struggles.

The group began meeting frequently, laying plans for the raid, which, because of the imminent sentencing of Philip and Tom Lewis for the earlier raid, had to take place sometime before May 27. Scouting around the Virginia, Maryland, and District of Columbia area, the members decided on the small, middle-class Maryland suburb of Catonsville. For their purpose, it was the perfect target. The Knights of Columbus Hall, where the local draft board had its office, was an easily accessible building. Of more importance, Catonsville, with its pleasant, tree-lined streets and moderately luxurious homes, seemed to them to be a symbol of the sort of community that through its complacent silence unwittingly endorsed government policies. The raid would be for the benefit of Catonsville's citizens as much as it was for the Vietnamese and other victims of war, racism, and poverty. The group greatly enjoyed the prospect of delivering a sizable jolt to the town's middle-class sensibilities.

Tom Lewis went to work drawing up a detailed plan of the interior setup of the Knights of Columbus Hall while his friends studied other tactical considerations. What, for instance, was to be the method of destroying the files? To Philip, Tom Lewis, and the others who had observed the reaction to the Baltimore raid, it seemed that the blood-pouring, in the end, had failed to serve its purpose. The average American had totally missed the liturgical significance of the blood. Philip suggested a method whose significance every American would recognize. Napalm is a chemical jelly composed largely of gasoline and soap. When ignited, this sticky substance is almost impossible to extinguish. The liberal use of napalm by the U.S. forces in Vietnam against its opponents horrified many people at home. Once dropped, usually from an airplane or helicopter, napalm spreads over a wide area and doesn't select its victims. Photos of savage burns on Vietnamese children arriving at American clinics revolted millions of citizens. Philip's suggestion was unanimously accepted. Taking a recipe for homemade napalm from the left-wing, Catholic-oriented magazine, *Ramparts*, the group mixed up a trial batch. It burned well.

Now the participants, the target, the method, and the date, May 17, were set. But for Philip, one very important and necessary ingredient was still missing: his brother Daniel.

Since Daniel's arrest at the Pentagon and Philip's guerrilla action in Baltimore, Daniel had been in conflict about which path to take. His had been one of the few voices raised in wholehearted support of Philip's raid, and he had agonized endlessly over Philip's approaching prison term. In early December, he elaborated on Philip's criticism of the Catholic Peace Fellowship. In a letter to James Forest and his friends at the CPF, he wrote: "All this is very painful to me because it is so personal; one has experiences, such as jailings and the threats of jail to those we love, and becomes convinced that *equivalent risk* is going to be the only source of community worth talking about. And that 'expressive' acts, such as Phil's, once they are thoughtful and proceed from a sacrificing heart, must be multiplied. And the masses may catch up as they wish, or not." The idea of "equivalent risk" was coming to have a great importance to Daniel, and in his discussions with friends he found himself using the term more and more frequently. He was proud of his brother. But what of Daniel's own role?

In the midst of preparation for Philip's trial, the long-awaited invitation from North Vietnam arrived. Together with Howard Zinn, a professor of history at Boston University and a radical opponent of the war, Daniel began the journey to North Vietnam to accept the release of three U.S. officers whose planes had been shot down while on bombing runs. The Tet offensive had just been launched by the National Liberation Front in the south and the two antiwar representatives were delayed in reaching Hanoi, but after a few days of waiting in Vientiane, Laos, a carefully planned flight took them to the North Vietnamese capital. They were met at the Hanoi airfield by members of the North Vietnamese Peace Committee, a smiling group of young men and women who greeted them with two bouquets of flowers. To Daniel it was a shock to be received with such warmth and courtesy by a people who had endured three years of intense bombing by his own countrymen. But the candor and lack of animosity on the part of the North Vietnamese continued throughout their stay. They spent five days touring Hanoi and its outskirts, meeting with workers and intellectuals, political leaders and soldiers. The two were often asked about Philip Berrigan, whose exploits were well known to the North Vietnamese and who they were overjoyed to learn was Daniel's brother. While in North Vietnam Daniel and Zinn accompanied the rest of the population into air raid shelters as American bombers blasted targets below. This close look at a besieged country gave Daniel an even deeper understanding of the war. When he returned to New York he told his friends: "I've graduated from innocence."

The April trial of Philip and his three codefendants brought Philip's sacrifice home even harder. Sitting in court as a spectator, Daniel watched his brother on the witness stand. Daniel felt strange and alienated as he, the guiltless, watched his brother, the guilty, tried for the crimes. He realized there was now a gap between Philip and himself, and wondered whether it could be closed again.

At Eastertime another factor was added to his considerations: A young high school boy, a Catholic, in nearby Syracuse, burned himself to death intentionally as Roger Laporte had done two years before. Speaking of it at the trial of the Catonsville Nine, Daniel said: "This boy had come to a point of despair about the war. He had gone into a Catholic cathedral, drenched himself with kerosene and immolated himself in the street. He was still living a month later when I was able to gain access to him. I smelled the odor of burning flesh and I understood anew what I had seen in North Vietnam. The boy was dying in torment, his body like a piece of meat cast upon a grille. He died shortly thereafter. I felt my sense had been invaded in a new way. I knew I must speak and act against death because this boy's death was being multiplied a thousandfold in the land of burning children."

But even as he stiffened his resolve to put his life on the line, something held him back. His friends began noticing a distinct change in him—he was brooding and unsmiling most of the time, very unlike the Daniel Berrigan they knew. An ulcer developed and he sought medical help for it, to no avail. But Philip Berrigan was determined to bring him in on the Catonsville action.

On May 12, in the early evening, Philip and two others from the group planning the raid arrived at Daniel's home in Ithaca. They found Daniel a little apprehensive about the subject of conversation—Catonsville. After several hours of discussion during which Daniel put up a stiff argument against his own participation, the two members of the raiding group left Philip and Daniel alone.

They spoke together as they had not for a long time.

Philip enumerated the reasons for the escalation in tactics as he had already done in numerous letters to Daniel. Daniel countered Philip's arguments as well as he could. Even if the action was morally correct and necessary, Daniel protested, wouldn't it in the end serve the purpose of the war's advocates? Wasn't there a place for a secondary leadership that would remain out of jail and continue the struggle? It was a battle waged countless times before, between men of thought and men of action. The contents of the bottle of rye on the table between them progressively diminished until the bottle was empty. As the night gradually lightened into dawn, Daniel found it impossible to escape the logic of Philip's conclusions. In the early morning Philip phoned George Mische to tell him simply, "Dan's in."

Daniel described his change of attitude at the trial: "I saw suddenly and it struck with the force of lightning, that my position was false, that I was threatened with verbalizing my moral substance out of existence. . . . Although I was too old to carry a draft card, there were other ways of getting in trouble with a state that seemed bent on multiplying the dead." The move cemented the bond between the brothers. Philip was overjoyed to have Daniel at his side and Daniel was happy and relieved to be there at last.

The night before the raid the group held one last strategy meeting. Their home-brewed napalm had been tested and retested to avoid all risk of accident and to forestall any chance of failure. They had gone over Tom Lewis's detailed drawing of the draft board office numerous times, but like commandos before a dangerous mission, they went over it once more. The newest member of the raiding party sat quietly next to Philip, staring with puzzlement at the intricate plan that had been handed to him. Displaying the qualities that had made him so effective as a field officer, Philip repeated the important instructions two or three times until sure he was understood. At the close of the meeting, the drawing still clenched in his hand, Daniel turned to his brother and said: "I didn't understand anything, Philly . . . never could read a map. I'll follow you, Philly, okay? I'll just follow you."

The night was spent at the house of a friend just a few miles from the morning's target. According to plan, a supporter of the group was to assemble a number of previously invited reporters at a motel. There they were given sealed envelopes and instructed not to open them until the word was given. One reporter from a Washington paper was delayed, and Philip paced about the suburban home where the group was waiting, berating the tardy reporter, until the telephone call finally came announcing that all was set with the press. Philip charged out of the house, jumped behind the wheel of a station wagon, and started to drive off. Then he realized he was alone in the car and screeched to a halt. The rest of the group spent a minute calming him down, then got into the three cars and took off.

The raid took less than three minutes. Looking out the window of their second-floor office, the draft board clerks, still in shock from the invasion moments before, saw the raiders assembled about the fire in the parking lot below. It was a bizarre scene. The group that had just swarmed shouting through the office now stood calmly with heads bowed and hands joined, many of them wearing smiles of satisfaction and relief. In a busy outer circle, reporters, TV cameramen, and photographers danced about snapping pictures, taking notes, and focusing their shoulder-mounted television cameras at the two men dressed in black who cut such different figures in their clerical attire.

In keeping with the religious tone of the attack, Daniel had prepared a meditation to accompany the statement. It was not until their trial, months later, that he was able to air it publicly.

. . . Our apologies, good friends, for the fracture of good order. The burning of paper, instead of children. . . . For we are sick at heart, our hearts give us no rest for thinking of the Land of Burning Children. . . . We say: killing is disorder, life and gentleness and community and unselfishness is the only order we recognize. For the sake of that order, we risk our liberty, our good name. The time is past when good men may be silent. . . . When, at what point, will you say no to this war? We have chosen to say with the gift of our liberty, if necessary our lives: the violence stops here. The death stops here. The suppression of truth stops here. This war stops here. . . .

On October 27, 1967, the Reverend Philip Berrigan poured blood on draft records at Selective Service headquarters in Baltimore, Maryland, to protest the Vietnam war. *Wide World Photos*

Philip Berrigan was handcuffed and taken to FBI headquarters following his arrest in St. Gregory's Church in New York City on April 21, 1970. *Wide World Photos*

LEFT Philip Berrigan (left) and Daniel Berrigan (right) were arrested on May 17, 1968, after participating in the burning of draft records removed from the Selective Service office in Catonsville, Maryland. *United Press International Photo*

On April 2, 1972, Daniel Berrigan left the federal building in Harrisburg, Pennsylvania, with Eqbal Ahmad and Sister Elizabeth McAlister, who were then being tried on conspiracy charges. *Wide World Photos*

LEFT The handcuffed but smiling Daniel Berrigan was taken into the Federal Building in Providence, Rhode Island, following his arrest by FBI agents on Block Island on August 11, 1970. *Wide World Photos*

Father Daniel Berrigan spoke to followers from the side door of New York's St. Patrick's Cathedral on June 4, 1972, after being forbidden to speak at a Mass for Peace inside. *Wide World Photos*

RIGHT Daniel and Philip Berrigan held a "resistance liturgy" in Danbury to celebrate Philip's release from the prison on December 20, 1972. *Wide World Photos*

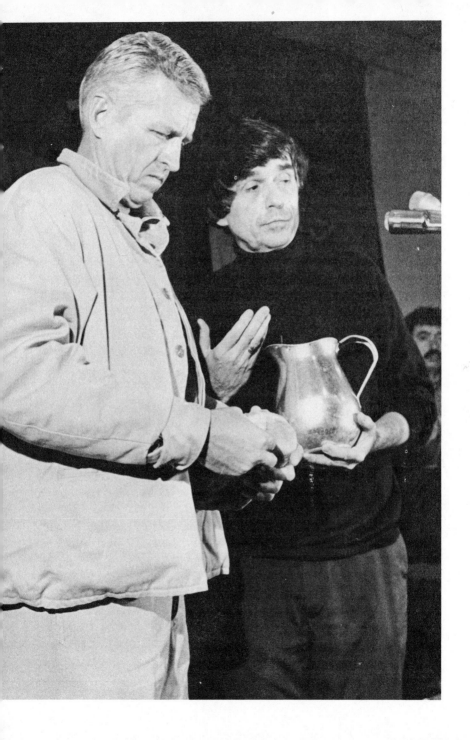

Philip and Daniel Berrigan walked arm-in-arm from the Federal
Correctional Institution at Danbury, Connecticut, following
Philip's release on parole. *Wide World Photos*

9

Seven of the Catonsville raiders were allowed to go free on bail, but Philip and Tom Lewis, having repeated the crimes of the previous October, were deemed too dangerous to remain at large and were held in federal prison. For many weeks Daniel fretted over his freedom while his brother was locked away, but gradually came to view his own freedom as a way for Philip also to be free—as if he were an extension of Philip's self through which all the pleasures and joys of life outside the prison walls could flow. The ulcer symptoms that had plagued Daniel in the months before the raid had vanished. He joked with friends about sending the medical bills he'd incurred to the White House. "It was their ulcer—not mine," he told them. All the guilt and self-doubt that had weighed so heavily upon him was gone. He returned to his work at Cornell with new zest and happiness.

Among many of his students at the university he was revered practically as a saint for his participation at Catonsville. The local chapter of the Students for a Democratic Society (SDS) regarded him as the truest radical on campus. Throughout the antiwar movement the reaction to Catonsville was far more favorable than it had been following the October raid in Baltimore. The difference lay not in the fact that the raids were unlike in character, but in the acceptance of the kind of resistance that the Berrigans represented. The peace talks in Paris had settled into a mire of disagreement from which they were not to emerge, and the

93

bitter fact that the war was continuing made many reconsider their earlier disagreements with the Berrigan style of public witness.

James Forest, in Los Angeles visiting various peace organizations, was filled with elation and wonder when he saw the photograph of the nine people at Catonsville on the front page of a Los Angeles paper. "There was Dan Berrigan, who'd been closer to me than any other man in my life, and Phil Berrigan, putting his life on the line for the second time in a row!" For Forest, who had criticized the Baltimore blood-pouring, the Catonsville raid demanded a reevaluation of his priorities. The message Philip had hoped to convey through his first action was finally getting across, and his wish for others to follow through with similar actions began to come true.

In Milwaukee, where a new Catholic Worker movement had just started, the Catonsville raid had the effect of a long-waited jolt into action. Along with Forest and Robert Cunane, a Catholic activist who had known Philip for many years, a small group of activists decided to follow his lead and make a foray into a Milwaukee draft board. On September 24, 1968, fourteen men, among them five Catholic priests and a Protestant minister, removed over ten thousand 1-A draft files from the headquarters of the Milwaukee Selective Service boards. In a nearby square where a monument honoring America's war dead stands, the raiders burned them with homemade napalm. The action, inspired by the witness of the Baltimore Four and the Catonsville Nine, went beyond the earlier raids in both size and scope. The destruction of ten thousand files containing all the information on Milwaukee's draft eligibles created chaos in the draft process of that city.

By the time the trial of the Catonsville Nine convened on October 7, it was clear that the government was no longer faced with the isolated actions of a few zealous activists. The spirit, purpose, and commitment of the Berrigans had caught on.

The Baltimore Defense Committee, a coalition of Baltimore peace groups, invited the people of America to attend the trial. This brought a response of over two thousand people who held marches, demonstrations, and rallies throughout that October week. It was the first time in many years that a trial had been the subject of so much passion and concern. To deal with the implied threat of thousands of antiwar protesters gathered in the city, Spiro Agnew, then governor of Maryland, requested an additional two hundred federal marshals to keep the demonstrations in line. Night after night the assemblage of students, priests, seminarians, nuns, ministers of the major Protestant sects, and the working people of Philip's Baltimore parish marched down Calvert Street to rally in front of the courthouse. Baltimore police, armed with gas masks, batons, helmets, and dogs, stood shoulder to shoulder along the route of the march. It took no great political wisdom to conclude that this was not an ordinary trial.

"All rise!" barked the bailiff as Federal Judge Roszel Thomsen entered the packed courtroom in long black robes. The roomful of people, the vast majority of them ardent supporters of the defendants, obediently stood. The jury, sworn in the day before, rose and faced the judge. The prosecution team, headed by a thin, young black man presenting his first political case, began to introduce the testimony and evidence for the government. The charred remains of 378 draft files were introduced as evidence, and draft board clerks were called as witnesses. But the defense did not contest this evidence. The nine defendants freely admitted they had committed the acts they were charged with, in fact assured the court they were glad they had done it. At issue was a question of much greater importance and urgency, a matter the government refused to consider: Why had they done it?

One by one, the counsels for the defense called the defendants to the witness stand to explain their reasons. David Darst was the first to be called. Twenty-six years old, well groomed, with an almost cherubic face, Darst was a prize student who had recently been offered a scholarship to the prestigious Harvard Divinity School. His parents sat in the front row of the courtroom, looking on with pride as their son recounted in a straightforward manner what had brought him to Catonsville on that bright May day.

". . . I suppose my thinking is part of an ethic found in the New Testament," he stated. "You could say Jesus too was guilty of assault and battery when he cast the money-changers out of the temple. . . . He was saying, It is wrong to do what you are doing, and this was our point: We have cried out on behalf of life. The government has chosen to see our cry as anarchy and arrogance. Perhaps the real anarchy lies in the acts of those who loose this plague of war. . . ."

Thomas Melville followed Darst onto the stand. A thick-set man with closely cropped hair, Melville told of his experience in Guatemala with the Maryknoll Mission, of the contradictions he had discovered between the proclaimed policy of the government and the reality of the life of the Guatemalan peasants. In describing their condition, Melville said: "I hesitate to use the word poverty—they were living in utter misery." He had tried to raise money to help form peasant cooperatives, even placing Church money as collateral for bank loans, much to the anger of his order when he was discovered. He had met with the president of Guatemala to plead with him to give land to the landless peasants but was politely refused, the president stating that there simply was no land to give them. It was at that point,

Melville testified, that he began to investigate recent Guatemalan history and discovered how the legally elected president of that country in 1954, Jacobo Árbenz Gúzman, was overthrown through the work of the Central Intelligence Agency when he attempted to seize land from the U.S.–controlled United Fruit Company. Melville's order had grown uneasy about his work with the peasants, and in 1967 he and Marjorie Melville, at that time a nun, were ordered out of the country. Melville's testimony was repeatedly interrupted by objections from the prosecution and from the judge, who insisted, "We are not trying the series of Guatemalan revolutions." But Melville continued: "We wanted to participate in the revolutionary movement. We knew it would not look good if an American priest or nun were killed in Guatemala by American Green Berets. We wanted to complicate things for the United States in Guatemala, because we did not want to see a slaughter there like the one in Vietnam...."

Marjorie Melville next gave her story. "On my return to the U.S. I was very happy when I found other people in this country concerned as I was. I know that burning draft files is not an effective way to stop a war, but who has found a way?" Short, pretty, and almost elegant in the way she addressed the court, Marjorie Melville was hardly the image of a hardened anarchist, as the prosecution had tried to portray her and her codefendants. She said: "I began to realize that my country's involvement in Guatemala was much deeper than what I had expected. Several times we asked for help from the Alliance for Progress ... they were very simple projects like putting water in a village ... we found out that funds were not available for these things. I found out later that ... the Alliance for Progress was giving all the anti-guerilla police in the cities new police cars. ..."
The prosecution pleaded with the judge to restrict testimony to the events at Catonsville, and Judge Thomsen or-

dered her to do so. However, the former nun persisted.

Mary Moylan, the other woman member of the Catonsville Nine, was the next to give her testimony. Thirty-two years old, a registered nurse who had spent six years in Uganda as a lay worker in a Catholic religious order—the White Sisters of Africa—Mary Moylan seemed no more radical than the women serving on the jury. But as she presented her story, the differences became apparent. After an incident in 1965, when American planes, piloted by Cubans, bombed Uganda, supposedly by accident, she had become interested in American foreign policy, a study that led her to question some of the practices of her order. After numerous disputes with her superiors, she was told to leave. Returning to America, she had gone to work for an organization of women volunteers in Washington, D.C., and had pursued her study of foreign policy. During that time she had become aware of the struggles in Washington's militant black community: "In Washington, a black youth was shot by a white policeman. A verdict of justifiable homicide was handed down. I remember too, a protest staged by a young leader who had a juvenile record. A southern congressman then read into the *Congressional Record* this man's juvenile record. This is absolutely forbidden by law. It was pointed out to the congressman that his procedure was illegal. His answer was, 'I did it once and I'll do it again.' . . . It became obvious to me that our politicians were right: Our foreign policy is indeed a reflection of our domestic policy. . . . To a nurse the effect of napalm on human beings is apparent. I think of children and women bombed by napalm, burned alive by a substance which does not roll off. . . . This is inhuman. . . . To pour napalm on pieces of paper is certainly preferable to using napalm on human beings. By pouring napalm on draft files I wish to celebrate life, not to engage in a dance of death."

George Mische, his hard eyes frowning and his jutting

chin pointing toward the defense counsel in front of him, began his testimony: "I worked in Central America and in the Caribbean. I organized labor groups, housing programs. . . . I went to Latin America with the idea that the Latins would be there waiting at the boat to greet me, because I was an American. This is the naivete we have, I guess, until we arrive overseas. . . . We were not only unwelcome, now and then we had bricks thrown at us. This confused me, but after I became involved at a higher level I began to understand." Mische ran down the list of the countries he had worked in, told of the corrupt dictatorships that were supported by the U.S. government through arms and aid. He talked hurriedly, as though he was afraid he'd be cut off before he could finish. At one point the chief prosecuting attorney leaped to his feet. "I have to object. I am trying to be patient, but I would suggest that we get to the issues." But to the Catonsville Nine, these *were* the issues. The government desperately wanted to make a simple case for lawbreaking, but as the defendants continued to parade to the witness stand it was clear that this was to be no simple matter.

John Hogan, friend and coworker of the Melvilles, began his testimony with a comparison: "If there were a group of children walking along the street, returning from school, and a car comes down the street out of control, even though there was a driver in that car, if I could divert the car from crashing into those children, I would feel an obligation to do so. Of course, the car is property and would be damaged. It is even possible that something would happen to the individual in the car. But no matter. I would be thinking ten times more of those children than of the driver of that car. And I know too, if I were the driver of that car, and it were out of control, I would hope and pray to God that somebody would smash my car so that I might not destroy those children."

The attorney for the defense asked Hogan to sum up in one phrase what his intention was in going to Catonsville. "I just want to let people live," Hogan replied. "That's all."

Tom Lewis, artist and activist, took the stand. A heavy blondish beard surrounding his large face, Lewis, like his close friend Philip Berrigan, had been a football star in his high school days and had given up the offer of a sports scholarship to college to attend art school in Italy. In 1965, when his brother was sent to Vietnam, he had begun to question the war, and when Pope Paul VI called the war a "war of genocide" he had begun actively to protest it. He spoke of his work in the Baltimore ghetto and then described the Baltimore Interfaith Peace Mission, which he had helped to found. As he related his reasons for his participation in both draft board raids, the judge became impatient. "I am obligated as a Christian to the primary law of brotherhood," Lewis went on. "Men have responsibilities not only to their immediate families but to the world."

"Yes, you've said that," snapped Judge Thomsen.

"So I made a decision to protest," Lewis continued. "This protest involved the pouring of blood—a strong indictment of those records—blood, in Biblical terms, is a symbol of reconciliation and related to the blood in Vietnam which is being wasted. Not only American blood, but the blood of the Vietnamese." Explaining his reasons for going ahead with a second act of civil disobedience while awaiting sentence for the first, Lewis told the court: "It was a choice between life and death. In a very Christian sense, it was a choice for saving a man's soul."

When the judge adjourned the trial for lunch, the defendants were swarmed over by their admirers. A serious-faced young Jesuit asked defense attorney William Kunstler why he thought the judge was permitting so much "extraneous" testimony to be read into the record. At the trial of Dr. Benjamin Spock, just a month before, the government had refused to allow the defendants to make any statements on their beliefs or their motives. "It's just possible," answered Kunstler, smiling thinly, "that he's passionately interested in what these defendants have to say."

When Philip Berrigan took the stand later that afternoon, the courtroom was tense and hushed. Philip, who along with Tom Lewis was led into the courtroom in handcuffs every morning, had been in jail for the previous six months. The signs of fatigue and strain were evident on his face as he started speaking. He spoke of his early years, of the experiences that had shaped him and started him on the road to Catonsville. Unlike those who had testified before him, Philip seemed uninterested in the proceedings. Gazing somewhere above the heads in the crowded room, his voice sounded like that of someone resigned to his fate. The partisan crowd leaned forward in their seats as though trying to prop him up and give him support.

He told of his army years, of the European cities blasted to rubble, of his early struggle against racism as a young priest in the Deep South, of the barriers thrown in his way by his own Church as he attempted to make the Gospel real in a real world, of his horror at the devastating possibility of nuclear war, the attempts to communicate the story of Vietnam to a community that did not want to listen, of his first hesitant protests against the war, protests that gradually grew into the realization that only a powerful nonviolent witness such as Baltimore or Catonsville could confront the powers that make war. "We have been accused of arrogance," Philip said, and some of the power of the giant priest began returning to his voice, "but what of the fantastic arrogance of our leaders? What of their crimes against the people, the poor and the powerless? Still, no court will try them, no jail will receive them. They live in righteousness. They will die in honor. For them we have one message, for those in whose manicured hands the power of the land lies. We say to them: Lead us. Lead us in justice and there will be no need to break the law. Let the president do what his predecessors failed to do. Let him obey the rich less, and the people more. Let him think less of the privileged and more of the poor, less of America and more of the world. Let the lawmakers, the judges and lawyers think less of the law and more of justice, less of legal ritual and more of human rights. . . ." The witness was excused. Philip stepped down from the stand and walked to the defendants' table. He clapped his hand on his brother's shoulder as Daniel rose to take the stand.

Defense counsel Harrup Freeman, a Quaker who taught law at Cornell, began the testimony with a question to Daniel about the effect of Philip's Baltimore raid on him. "I began to understand," Daniel answered, "one could not indefinitely obey the law while social conditions deteriorated, structures of compassion breaking down, neighborhoods slowly rotting, the poor despairing. . . . My brother's action helped me to realize that from the beginning of our Republic good men had said no, acted outside the law when conditions so demanded. And if a man did this, time might vindicate him—show his act to be lawful. . . . A few men must have a long view, must leave history to itself to interpret their lives. . . ." Freeman then asked Daniel about his intent in burning the files. "I did not want the children, or the grandchildren of the jury or the judge, to be burned with napalm."

The judge sat up at Daniel's remark. "You say your intention was to save these children, of the jury, of myself, when you burned those records? That's what I heard you say. I ask you if you meant that."

"I meant that," Daniel replied, "of course I meant that, or I would not say it. . . ."

"You cannot think up arguments now that you would

have liked to have had on your mind then," the judge countered.

"My intention on that day," Daniel began again, "was to save the innocent from death by fire. I was trying to save the poor who are mainly charged with dying in this war. I poured napalm on behalf of the prosecutor's and the jury's children. It seems to me quite logical. If my way of putting facts is inadmissible, then so be it. . . ."

It was an example of the lack of communication that was to continue throughout Daniel's testimony. As he repeated some of the facts and experiences of his life, the judge often stopped him, asking him to repeat or explain. At the close of Daniel's testimony the defense rested its case.

On the next day, the government and the defense summarized their cases for the jury. First, the prosecuting attorney attempted to belittle the testimony of the defendants. "Among these nine defendants there are four or five justifications floating around," the attorney claimed. "One defendant is upset about one ill in the world, and that justifies *his* going to Catonsville. Another is upset about another ill in the world and that justifies *his* going to Catonsville. And so on. There could be fifty defendants, each upset about different supposed ills in the world. And each one of them could say: 'This is why I violated the law.'" The government advocate went on to reassure the jury that everyone knew the country wasn't perfect but that things would eventually get better. "But our problems are not going to be solved by people who deliberately violate our laws, the foundation and support for an ordered and just and civilized society."

William Kunstler approached the jury to present the case for the defense. He suggested to them that this was an historic moment, that the case before them was not a simple one of a group of people burning something that belonged to the government. He invoked the trials of Socrates and

Jesus as parallels. The Catonsville Nine, he said, "were trying to make an outcry, to reach the American community before it was too late. I think this is an element of free speech to try—when all else fails—to reach the community." When Kunstler had finished, Judge Thomsen ordered an adjournment before giving his instructions to the jury. The supporters of the defendants walked out of the courtroom and into the corridor outside. Dozens waited outside to discuss the case and predict its outcome. But to the great majority, the outcome was already a foregone conclusion.

When the court reconvened early on the afternoon of October 10, the judge instructed the jury to forget all it had heard during the defendants' testimony. "The law does not recognize political, or religious or moral reasons or some higher law as justification for the committing of a crime," he informed them. He admitted that the protesters might even be right in the eyes of history, but this had no bearing on how the jury was to weigh the case. As the judge was charging the jury, a number of federal marshals began filing into the room, until they lined the entire side and rear walls of the court. The government had become nervous about an outburst. The authorities had been pleased that so far there had been no outbreaks of violence and they didn't want their record spoiled now.

When Judge Thomsen had finished his instructions to the jury, the members stood and quietly walked single file through a small door at the end of the jury box. William Kunstler rose and stepped up to the judge. "Your honor," he said, "the defendants have requested to be permitted to say something to the court." It was an unheard-of request and the judge's consent was even more amazing. The courtroom hummed with whispered conversations. Judge Thomsen rapped his gavel and requested order. "I want to hear the defendants, I do not want to cut them off from anything they may want to say," he said.

For forty minutes there was a polite conversation between the judge and the defendants. The prosecution team sat at their table openmouthed in amazement as Daniel Berrigan said to the court: "It is our soul that has brought us here, it is our soul that has got us into trouble. It is our conception of man. We really cannot be dismembered in such a way that it can be found eventually that our cadavers are here, and our soul is elsewhere, and our moral passion is outside the consideration of this court, as though the legal process is an autopsy on us."

The judge looked down at Daniel Berrigan. "Well, I cannot match your poetic language," he said, and there was a burst of applause from the audience. Banging his gavel repeatedly, Judge Thomsen threatened to clear the court if there were any further outbreaks. When the room had calmed, he continued speaking. "I think you all for some reason . . . simply do not understand the function of this court. . . ." He spoke of his role as a judge and of the actions of the defendants. He cautioned them that had they done what they did in certain other countries they would not have been tried at all, but simply executed. But Daniel had not finished.

"Your honor, you spoke very movingly of your understanding of what it is to be a judge. I wish to ask whether or not reverence for the law does not also require a judge to interpret and adjust the law to the needs of the people here and now . . . it may be possible, even though the law excludes certain important questions of conscience, to include them none the less; and thereby to bring the tradition to life again for the sake of the people." It was the quietest moment since the trial had begun. Judge Thomsen suddenly looked terribly weary. He removed his glasses and polished them with a cloth. As he spoke to Daniel he sounded very different from the moment before.

"You speak to me as a man and as a judge," he said quietly, "I would be a funny sort if I were not moved by your sincerity on the stand, and by your views. I agree with you completely, as a person. We can never accomplish, or give a better life to people, if we are going to keep on giving so much money to war. It is very unfortunate but the issue of war cannot be presented as clearly as you would like. The basic principle of the law is that we do things in an orderly fashion. People cannot take the law into their own hands."

The astonishing exchange between the accused and the man who sat in judgment of them continued. Philip Berrigan spoke up. "Your honor," he began, "I think we would be less than honest with you if we did not state our attitude. Simply, we have lost confidence in the institutions of this country, including our church. I think this has been a rational conclusion on our part. We have come to our conclusion slowly and painfully. We have lost confidence because we do not believe these institutions are reformable."

"If you say that," Judge Thomsen answered, "then you are advocating revolution."

Daniel Berrigan thanked the judge for speaking with them and made one last request. "Could we finish with a prayer? We would like to recite the 'Our Father' with our friends." Though this procedure, too, was unheard of the judge offered no objections. The entire court—prosecution, defendants, judge, jury, marshals, stenographer, and spectators stood and repeated the Our Father slowly and reverently.

Almost two hours later the jury announced it had reached a verdict. One by one the jurors were queried as to their decisions. Each quietly pronounced, "Guilty."

As the last of these responses echoed through the room, a member of the audience cried from the rear of the court, "Members of the jury, you have just found Jesus Christ guilty." The judge ordered the courtroom cleared. He turned once more to the defendants and asked if they had anything further to say. "We would simply like to thank the Court and the prosecution," Daniel replied. "We agree that this is the greatest day of our lives."

The supporters of the nine were waiting for them when they emerged from the courthouse. As they came down the long steps, friends and admirers rushed up to meet them while behind them a three-deep cordon of helmeted riot police closed off the courthouse from further access. But the protesters and the defendants barely noticed. Daniel and Philip, surrounded by nuns and priests, many of whom had been in Baltimore during the week to show their support, still wore the ironic smiles of triumph that had spread over their faces as the verdict was read.

A month later the Catonsville Nine returned to the same courthouse to be sentenced. Several hundred people accompanied them and rallied outside while Judge Thomsen read the sentences. David Darst, John Hogan, Marjorie Melville, and Mary Moylan were each given two years; George Mische, Thomas Melville, and Daniel Berrigan, three. Philip Berrigan and Tom Lewis received sentences of three and a half years, to run concurrently with the six-year sentence they had previously received. Pending appeal, all save Philip and Lewis were allowed to post bail, and six weeks later the remaining two were also allowed out on bail.

As everyone had expected, the defendants had been convicted, but the sentences were more lenient than many had feared they might be. And for the Catonsville Nine there had been moments in the trial when the truth had been heard and the people had listened. They had never expected that the court would acquit them; what had been more important was that their crimes were international knowledge, and they had informed the entire nation of their beliefs and principles. From the millions of people who had followed the proceedings at the federal courthouse in Baltimore, to the thousands who had rallied in the Baltimore streets to defend and support the nonviolent resisters, to the judge, who, in a moment of respite from the bitter politics of the case, had been moved by the testament of the Catonsville Nine, countless people had been reached. And a deep, if small, dent had been made in the armor of American militarism.

10

The wave of resistance that mounted with the Baltimore raid and then Catonsville continued to grow after the trial. The targets were mainly draft boards, and the style of the raids followed that set by the Berrigans. In Chicago over a hundred thousand files were destroyed in one protest led by Catholics, whose resistance was now a national phenomenon and, for the government and Church authorities, a most disturbing one.

Daniel and Philip, ebullient that their message was being heard and taken to heart across the country, remained out of prison through 1969 as they attempted to appeal their convictions. The Catonsville Nine busied themselves in raising funds for their defense and working in the support of other groups who had raided draft boards.

A great blow struck the defendants when David Darst was killed in an automobile crash. For Daniel and Philip, Darst's death was especially painful. The youngest of the nine defendants, Darst had at first been suspected of being a government plant. His keen desire to be a part of the planned action though he had never participated in a demonstration before had made Philip wonder at his genuineness. But he had rapidly discovered that Darst's intentions were every bit as sincere as his own. Darst had handed in four successive draft cards, and when released from jail after the Catonsville raid he was promptly imprisoned in Saint Louis for draft evasion. In prison again, he began a fast while waiting for his order, the Christian Brothers, to bail him out. The wait was in vain, as his superiors informed him that they wanted no part of his activities and he would have to cope by himself. A group of young Saint Louis resisters finally got bail money together and secured his release. Intent on continuing active resistance against the war, Darst was killed on a mission to visit the jailed members of the Milwaukee Fourteen.

When the Supreme Court refused to reconsider the verdict reached in Baltimore, the government set April 9, 1970, as the date for the remaining eight to begin serving their sentences. According to the civil disobedience philosophy of Gandhi, the nonviolent resister must voluntarily submit himself to the punishment imposed by the authorities. This pattern had been followed in the civil rights protests of the sixties. But in their travels across the country and their countless meetings with antiwar activists, some of the Catonsville Nine had come to question this concept. Why, they asked, should they voluntarily cut themselves off from the movement and the effectiveness of their voices? Wouldn't it be of more value to their cause to keep out of jail and stay active?

Evading the clutches of the FBI, however, meant going "underground"—a life of constant hiding, discomfort, and endless precautions. Members of the Students for a Democratic Society and the Black Panthers, a militant black organization, had already chosen this route in the face of severe jail terms. But unlike the communities that the Panthers and SDS relied on for support, the majority of the backers of the Catholic antiwar movement were middle-class people living in the mainstream of society. How could one remain hidden and still organize and agitate?

In late March, George Mische and Mary Moylan announced their intention to go underground. Refusing to accept jail, they reasoned, was parallel to refusal of induction into the armed forces—a principled decision to no longer accept the "order" imposed by the government. The two Berrigans, along with David Eberhardt of the Baltimore Four who had also been ordered to begin his sentence on April 9, spent long hours discussing what the results of such an act might be. In the end, they endorsed the idea of going underground in principle but decided on a different tactic they hoped would serve their cause even more. They would refuse to surrender themselves at the time and place the government had ordered. They would keep out of sight and safely hidden. In the meantime, they would publicly announce plans to appear at large antiwar rallies. This would serve as a public dare to the FBI: Come and get us, they would in effect be saying, but you'll have to snatch us in full view of thousands of our supporters!

April 9 came and went and Mische, Moylan, the Berrigans, and Eberhardt failed to appear as the law required. The Department of Justice promptly obtained bench warrants for their arrest and the matter was turned over to the FBI.

At Cornell, where Daniel had continued his work as cochairman of United Religious Work until April 9, a festival was planned for the weekend of April 16–17. Entitled "America Is Hard to Find," it was announced as a "freedom seder" that would include music, radical theater, discussion groups, and speeches. In late announcements of the festival, its organizers revealed their biggest calling card of all: The FBI's most wanted Jesuit, Cornell's own Daniel Berrigan, would address the flock on the evening of the seventeenth. Daniel had decided to "go with a bang!" by letting himself be captured on his own turf before his most stalwart supporters.

That night, the large hall at Cornell was packed with students, faculty, young Jesuits, seminarians, nuns, and reporters. Conspicuously interspersed among them were dozens of FBI agents and federal marshals. A loud commotion swelled into cheers and applause as Daniel, surrounded by a tightly knit group of student protectors, swept into the hall. The government agents balked at pouncing on Daniel then and there, fearing a violent reaction from the crowd. Their hesitation was to prove their undoing, and led to one of the worst public embarrassments ever suffered in the long career of their chief, J. Edgar Hoover.

Taking a seat on the stage, Daniel sat with a cheerful grin on his face as a student moved to the podium to introduce him. Around the sides of the stage immense papier-mâché figures representing the twelve apostles moved cumbrously back and forth. Part of the ongoing pageant, the figures were from the Bread and Puppet Theatre, which had performed earlier in the evening. The crowd quieted as Daniel approached the podium and began to speak. Briefly he recounted the action at Catonsville. He then asked the people thronged before him when they were going to move to resistance. The country needed them as never before, he said. He spoke loudly and with passion. It was to be the last time he would address a crowd for a very long time—his last message before jail, or so he thought. Once again the hall swelled with the cheers of students as he finished.

As Daniel resumed his seat, a voice whispered in his ear: "Want to split?" He turned to see a friend on the Cornell faculty seated behind him. In a hushed, but matter-of-fact tone, the friend continued: Daniel's departure could be quite simple—at a given signal the lights would dim and Daniel would slip under one of the large papier-mâché figures and leave the stage. Outside a pickup truck was waiting to spirit him away. "Give me ten minutes to think about it," the Jesuit replied and turned back to look over the audience.

He had already gone over in his mind many times what the reality of life underground might be like. He had agreed with Mische and Moylan's thesis that a good deal of constructive work could be carried out by a radical slipping in and out of communities across the nation. The idea of such an existence intrigued him. It was a chance for him to go on making the kind of political protests he deemed so vital. Even more alluring was the vision of escaping under the very noses of the federal agents scattered around the hall. It was the kind of childlike mischievousness that delighted him. With an impish smile, he turned back to his friend. "Sure—let's go," he said.

At a moment when a suddenly darkened hall could be accepted by the audience as part of the performance, the lights went off. When they came back on, one of the bloated papier-mâché figures was edging toward the stage exit door. No one noticed the black clergyman's trousers peeking from the bottom of the figure. In a moment the immense puppet had left the stage. Still inside the figure, Daniel was led out of the building and into the waiting pickup. The truck sped away from the campus. As it raced off into the night, Daniel Berrigan, the only priest ever to grace the FBI's most wanted list, began his four-month stretch as a fugitive from justice, or, as he liked to call it, a fugitive from injustice.

Inside the hall it had taken the government agents only an instant to notice that their quarry was no longer seated on the stage when the lights came back on. After a few minutes of racing about, they connected the exiting puppet with Daniel's escape and took off in pursuit. They found the pickup just a couple of miles away, abandoned.

Actually, the escape plan offered to Daniel in such an offhand way had been carefully planned and arranged: A car had been left not far from campus and the drivers and their cargo had switched vehicles to avoid detection. One of the FBI men was given the distasteful task of informing headquarters in Washington that Berrigan had appeared, but escaped again. Another was delegated the equally distasteful job of telling this to the many newspaper and TV reporters gathered to cover what they assumed was an impending arrest. For Hoover and his men it was not a good day.

Having been publicly embarrassed by Daniel's escape, the FBI had almost two hundred men posed at Saint Gregory's church in Manhattan on April 21 when it was announced that Philip and David Eberhardt would make an appearance there. There were high hopes in the bureau of capturing Daniel there as well.

Three days after his disappearance from the public light, Daniel met with Philip and George Mische, both, at that point, still "on the lam." Daniel told them he intended to stay underground for as long as he could manage. This was Mische's intention as well and they parted, not to see each other for many months.

Philip and Eberhardt spent the night of the twentieth at Saint Gregory's. Daniel went to the nearby convent of the religious order of the Sacred Heart of Mary where he was watched over by a close friend of Philip's, Sister Elizabeth McAlister, a woman who was to play an increasingly important role in Philip's and Daniel's lives. On the morning of April 21, a half-dozen FBI agents appeared at Saint Gregory's and demanded that the rector allow them to search the premises. The rector, sympathetic to Philip and Eberhardt and aware that they were hiding within, tried to stall the agents. He asked them if they had a search warrant. They brusquely informed him that there was no need of a specific warrant to search the church, as there was a standing bench warrant for the arrest of the felons. Searching the three floors of the building in pairs, the FBI men were determined to find and arrest the fugitives before the rally scheduled for that evening. No one at FBI headquarters wanted a repeat performance of Cornell.

Opening a closet door on the third floor, the agents found

Philip and Eberhardt. The two notorious draft record destroyers were handcuffed and led away.

Daniel, unaware that the FBI was about to search the rectory, had left for a safer hiding place just minutes before the agents appeared. While the two hundred agents scoured the rally that evening looking for the Berrigan still at large, Daniel was safely tucked away in New Jersey. At the rally, Dr. Eqbal Ahmad, a Pakistani radical who had worked with Daniel at Cornell, read the prepared remarks that Philip had intended to deliver in person. Frequently interrupted by loud and long bursts of applause, Philip's speech was received with the sort of reverence the movement reserves for its martyrs.

Daniel's escape into the Ithaca night was his attempt to break what he called "the unending ritual of crime and punishment." Through the late spring and summer of 1970 he moved from home to home, from town to city and back again. His route was carefully mapped out by Eqbal Ahmad, who arranged with dozens of middle-class families who had never met Daniel to shelter him for a short time and then aid in discreetly passing him on to his next stop. Harboring a fugitive from the law is a felony that carries a stiff sentence. But the people that Ahmad approached were pleased to have this particular fugitive as a guest, and honored that so much trust was placed in them. The potential consequences of the act put off very few.

In early May, the United States invaded Cambodia. The resulting outcry at home rocked the Nixon administration. A national student strike was called against the latest escalation, and on dozens of campuses police and the National Guard moved in to quell the uprisings. At Kent State University in Ohio four students were killed when National Guard troops fired into a group of protesters. Two of the victims were females and all were white and from middle-class families.

As Daniel began to circulate among the liberal professionals who offered their homes to him, he attempted to draw them into more active confrontations with the American "system." Many who have known both Daniel and Philip have said that one of their most potent weapons is their way of shaming people into action. To those outside their circle, their very presence seems to say: "I've put my life on the line—what are you doing?" It was a tactic that Daniel used most effectively during his fugitive period. The sudden escalation of the war and the Kent State killings had already shaken the liberals' world, and in the homes where Daniel was a guest he challenged his hosts to compare their lives with his. Playing with the children and helping with the household chores, in the evenings he would always bring the conversation around to the same point: commitment. He was seeking individuals to follow the examples of his brother, himself, and their friends. Most of the prosperous middle-class people with whom he stayed were too set in their ways, too caught up in obligations to children, careers, and material values to simply chuck them aside and follow him. But if he was disappointed he did not show it.

He pursued the same life-style he had done since his ordainment. Part of the day was reserved for reading and writing, while the morning hours were set aside for prayer and meditation. He was still very much a priest and felt that his present situation was a direct outgrowth of his priestly duties. But the reaction of the news media to his escape from Cornell was a source of great concern to him. Instead of treating Daniel's fugitive status as a serious political statement, the press referred to him as "the Catholic Robin Hood," as though he were merely out on a merry jaunt.

In an effort to publicize the solemn reasons for his escape, Daniel wrote articles for the *New York Review of Books* and *Saturday Review* and gave interviews to reporters from the *Village Voice*, the *New Yorker*, and the *New York Times*.

The articles elicited great sympathy for him and the ridicule was heard less often. His underground journeys and appearances were remarkably well organized. Daniel's ability to pop up and disappear again made the FBI appear slightly ludicrous to many people.

As the summer wore on, Daniel conceived the idea of giving a Sunday sermon in a Catholic cathedral. He would appear after the congregation had gathered and depart before the authorities could be summoned. Through friends, Daniel approached several liberal priests with this idea, but each refused, citing the dangers and possible bad publicity for their churches as reasons. Depressed by the unwillingness of his own churchmen to allow him in their midst, Daniel took the idea to Protestant churches. The chaplain of a small Methodist church outside Philadelphia expressed interest and the guest sermon was arranged.

There was no advance notice. At a Sunday morning service on August 2, 1970, after the minister had finished a reading from Paul's Epistle to the Hebrews, he announced that Daniel Berrigan, a distinguished Jesuit priest, would be giving the sermon of the day. Dressed in clerical attire, Daniel began speaking to the assemblage of prosperous Methodists. "I come to you," he began, "in the name of all those who have said no to this war, from prison, from the underground, from exile, from the law courts, from death itself." It was clear from the expressions on the faces of the congregation that they had not yet identified Daniel as the fugitive priest. But as he continued the sermon many heads turned aside and whispered. The passage read to them concerned itself with faith, a belief in something mightier than the temporal power of nature or kings. Speaking to the Hebrews, Paul had evoked the names of all the great Jews of the past who had suffered as a result of their faith in God. Daniel described them as "such witnesses to the truth as to become part of that truth itself, so that we may now hear their lives and deaths as God's word." He likened the times of the early Jews to the present, and asked people before him how they could apply the horrors of Vietnam to their own lives. As for himself, Daniel told them, the choice had already been made. There are hundreds of nonviolent means of opposing the war, he said, from harboring fugitives like himself to making it difficult for draft boards to operate. "The peace will not be won without such serious and constant and sacrificial and courageous actions on the part of large numbers of good men and women." It was a brief address. Daniel had presented the core of the Berrigan ethic —the call for a return to Christian sacrifice, to follow one's faith wherever it migh lead. Smiling at the congregation, he concluded: "May the peace of Christ, which is promised to the courageous and the patient and the cheerful of heart, be yours also." Stepping down from the pulpit, Daniel left through the minister's rectory. None of the congregation had left their seats during the sermon. There was a pay phone in the hallway. Any of the churchgoers could have walked to it and called the FBI. No one had. When the lean, smiling Jesuit was gone, the words of Paul's Epistle to the Hebrews hung over the room. "Who through faith subdued kingdoms, wrought righteousness, obtained promises, stopped the mouths of lions, quenched the violence of fire. . . ."

Daniel's "Sermon from the Underground," as that Sunday morning address was called, was reprinted and published in magazines around the country. A number of newspaper accounts of the fugitive's appearance were almost gleeful as they told of the ease with which Daniel had slipped in and out of the church and calmly offered his message of nonviolent resistance to a public assembly.

It proved to be Daniel's last public appearance before capture. The FBI, from its director to the men in the field, was smarting from its inability to locate the fugitive priest.

If Daniel was available to Edwin Newman for a televised interview broadcast to a prime-time audience, why could the FBI find no way to apprehend him? When Daniel, in one interview, referred to Hoover and his department as the "Keystone Kops," it was the last straw for the bureau that prided itself on its crime-stopping accomplishments. Daniel's apprehension was given top priority by Hoover himself, and dozens more agents were assigned to the task of finding him. But despite the increase in manpower and time and effort, it was only Daniel's recklessness, and a reference to his whereabouts contained in a note smuggled to Philip in prison, that finally tipped off the bureau.

All through Daniel's four-month jaunt, Eqbal Ahmad, who had assumed the task of finding him refuge and keeping the FBI off the scent, had pleaded with Daniel not to visit his old friends. But for a man who had built his life around throwing caution to the winds, the advice was too harsh to accept. A few days after the successful sermon, Daniel elected to visit his old and good friends, William Stringfellow and Anthony Towne, two retired writers and lawyers who shared a house on tiny Block Island.

Several miles off the Rhode Island coast, Block Island contains fewer than two hundred homes. Most of the residents are summer visitors from New York who get to the island by airplane or ferry. For a fugitive to seek safety on an island is a foolhardy act. When the FBI pieced together the information contained in a letter sent by Sister Elizabeth McAlister to Philip via an inmate who proved to be an informant, the capture of the elusive priest became a simple task.

On August 11, a Coast Guard cutter appeared in Block Island's harbor. Storm warnings were already out as a strong northeast gale blew across the island. In what was supposed to be a surreptitious entry, seventy FBI men landed at the airport. Dressed in orange rain slickers and carrying binoculars around their necks, the group told curious residents they were birdwatchers. This left the local people scratching their heads. Everyone (except the FBI, apparently) knew birds keep out of sight during stormy weather.

The agents set out for Eschaton, Stringfellow's and Towne's residence, but really had no need of even their flimsy cover story. The airport guarded, the harbor blockaded, there was no way for Daniel to leave the island short of submarine.

At Eschaton, Daniel, Stringfellow, and Towne had just finished a pleasant breakfast. The short stay had already relaxed Daniel considerably. The presence of friends and the easy conversation allowed him to forget for a moment the hardships of the previous months. The three friends were seated in the living room looking through magazines and newspapers when they became aware of the bright orange figures moving about near the house. There was no doubt who the prowlers might be.

When the agents had the house thoroughly surrounded, four of them approached the front door. Before they knocked, the door opened. In the entranceway stood Daniel Berrigan, a quiet smile on his face. Introducing himself to the visitors, Daniel stepped aside to let them in out of the rain. Handcuffs appeared and Daniel, after being allowed to don a rubber poncho, was shackled with hands in front of him. The underground sojourn had come to an end.

During the trip back to the mainland, one of the FBI agents, a serious young man with close-cropped hair, confided to Daniel that he, too, had been a Jesuit. "You know what I said to myself when I put the cuffs on you? I said, 'Ad Majorem Dei Gloriam' [the Jesuit slogan meaning 'To the Greater Glory of God']." Daniel looked at the agent sadly.

When the light plane carrying the priest and his arresting officers landed, a large group of reporters and photographers were on hand to record the scene. Still handcuffed, with two grim-faced agents holding him by the arms, Daniel threw his head back and flashed his most victorious smile. A photographer captured the moment. In the camera's eye, the sober, almost desperate-looking agents appeared as the conquered, the grinning priest the victor.

During his first week in prison, Daniel wrote to relatives: "No point in mourning. Though I did it myself at first. It is dreadful to think that good friends suffer. But how else will anything get accomplished? . . . Certainly for priests and nuns to be jailed is an honor in such days— it will be one of the few honors the Church can point to in days ahead."

Sent to the Federal Correctional Institution at Danbury, Connecticut, to serve his term, Daniel was elated at the news that Philip was to join him there. After Philip's and Eberhardt's capture hours before they'd intended to surrender, George Mische was the next to be apprehended, while in Chicago in late May. Mary Moylan, the nurse-turned-activist from Baltimore, remained at large. None of them had fled out of fear of the unpleasantness of jail, but for Philip and Eberhardt jail was proving far worse than they had anticipated.

After their April arrest they had been taken to Lewisburg Federal Penitentiary in Pennsylvania. Lewisburg is one of several maximum security prisons where inmates deemed dangerous or prone to escape are housed. It has a high, thick concrete wall running around it with gun turrets placed at strategic positions. All the safeguards are there— triple locks, sliding steel doors, guards on each cell block twenty-four hours a day. One section of the prison is called the "jungle" because there, in an immense dormitory, the most hardened inmates are placed. The mere threat of sending an inmate to the "jungle" is enough to calm the most rebellious prisoners. Since draft resisters and other so-called political prisoners had begun entering federal prisons in large numbers in the mid-sixties, Lewisburg was used as a processing point before sending them off to minimum security prisons such as nearby Allenwood, where prisoners are allowed to work out of doors and security is not nearly as strict. Philip, who had spent a large part of his seven months preceding the Catonsville trial at Allenwood, expected to be sent there within a few days of his arrival at Lewisburg. But these turned into weeks and then months.

Lewisburg is notorious for the number of slayings and beatings among its population. The danger of homosexual attack is also great. After a month at the maximum security prison, Philip began to suspect that he and Eberhardt were being held there because it was suspected they knew where his brother Daniel was hiding. Guards frequently tore apart Philip's cell looking for evidence. It is standard prison procedure to search cells for weapons or contraband, but the shakedowns of Philip's cell were carried out with rare care and detail and were an almost daily occurrence. David Eberhardt was kept in a cell with other prisoners who frequently taunted him and threatened to rape him. Eberhardt, quiet, shy, and peaceable, was unprepared for the hostility of his cellmates. When the threats became more frequent, he began to anticipate an attack momentarily. He got word to Philip, and together they managed to visit the prison chaplain. Soon, the guards discovered them and removed them back to their cells.

Hours later, they were informed that because they had broken prison regulations by being in an unauthorized section (and also because they had made the harmless mistake of waiting in the incorrect food line at dinner the evening before), they were to be denied recreation privileges for a week. It was a harsh punishment for such minor offenses and Philip and Eberhardt recognized it as part of the harassment they had been receiving since entering Lewisburg. They decided to enter solitary confinement and begin a fast to protest their treatment. Before entering solitary, Philip managed to send a letter to friends describing conditions at the prison and his and Eberhardt's treatment. In the letter he spoke of the routine "dehumanization of the inmates" and added that men imprisoned for their beliefs were treated even worse.

After two days of solitary, the guards came to release them. Eberhardt and Philip refused to go, stating that they intended to continue their fast and remain in solitary. The fasting became a source of concern to prison officials. The warden sent them to the hospital where they could be carefully observed. Philip, as was his right, sent a letter to Senator Charles Goodell of New York describing the situation. Goodell, known for his liberal sentiments, responded to Philip's plea and set in motion the chain of events that eventually secured the transfer of Philip and Eberhardt. But that took time.

Meanwhile, in the first weeks at Lewisburg, a young inmate named Boyd Douglas had approached Philip and expressed his sympathies with the antiwar movement. At first Philip reacted guardedly. Most of the inmates were staying clear of Philip. He was regarded as "hot." With a brother pursued by the FBI and the warden himself taking a special interest in his case, the older prisoners figured any association with the priest could mean trouble. So when Douglas appeared, Philip was suspicious. Taking care not to offend him, Philip went to other draft resisters held at Lewisburg and questioned them about the young inmate. The response was unanimous: Douglas was a good and trustworthy person—and of value to the resisters because he had access to the outer world. Under a study-release program, Douglas was allowed to attend nearby Bucknell University on a daily basis—he would leave Lewisburg at seven or eight o'clock in the morning and was on his own until five-thirty or six in the evening when he returned to the prison. Douglas thus had a perfect opportunity to send and receive messages. In his civil rights work and antiwar activities Philip was always a cautious person. But the hardship of his imprisonment at Lewisburg was taking its toll. As he had discovered, inmates were being urged to inform on him, his cell constantly scrutinized. For a man of Philip's enormous energy, the normal reactions to prison life were magnified a hundredfold. He very badly needed some connection with the outer world, someone he could trust. And so Douglas was taken into his confidence. This was an error that would result in Daniel's capture and a federal indictment against Philip and six others.

Philip prepared a letter to Sister Elizabeth McAlister. He described an inmate willing to transmit messages between them and suggested that she make trips to the Bucknell campus to meet with the "courier." In the letter he spoke of the possibility of organizing the inmates. When the letter, folded between the pages of *Newsweek*, was discovered by prison authorities, Philip was summoned to the warden's office. The suggestions of radicalizing the prison population outraged the prison official, as did the mention of beginning an illegal correspondence. The warden assured Philip that he knew exactly who the courier was, but Philip refused to believe him. As his punishment for writing the letter, Sister McAlister was taken off Philip's list of legal correspondents. When Philip returned to his cell he told Douglas of the discovery and the warden's remark that he knew what Douglas was planning to do. Boyd scoffed, and Philip decided to go ahead with his secret messages.

The next day, during a break between classes at Bucknell, Douglas met with two agents of the FBI. Telling them about his access to Philip, Douglas suggested they hire him as an informant. The FBI, eager to have inside information about the Catholic resistance, immediately agreed. From that point on, every message Philip sent to Elizabeth Mc-

Alister, and every one from her to Philip, was photocopied and handed over to the FBI.

As many ex-convicts have revealed, privacy in prison is won only by a constant battle. A correspondence that does not have to go through the prison mailroom is a precious thing, for in the mailroom, normal correspondence is read aloud by the censors and guards, often laughed over and handed around. So when Philip made the agreement with Douglas, he clung to the letters he wrote to and received from Elizabeth McAlister as if they were a lifeline. They were immensely personal and never intended to go beyond themselves, for they contained thoughts neither of them would have revealed in public. As it developed, their letters were being read as openly as magazines.

As Douglas dutifully continued to carry messages between the two, their relationship became stronger. Douglas pretended to be avidly interested in resistance and told Philip he wanted to become more involved when he was released. Philip took him further into his confidence. He told the aspiring activist of his dissatisfaction with the anti-war movement, and mentioned to him one or two plans that had been in the works before his capture. On an afternoon in late February, 1970, Philip had gone with Father Joseph Wenderoth, an active member of the Baltimore resistance community, to a government building in Washington, D.C. Posing as government engineers, they had slipped past the guards and gained access to the heating ducts that form miles of endless tunnels beneath official Washington. The plan in mind, as they walked through the dusty, steamy tunnels, was to somehow, probably with an explosive device, knock out the heating system for all government buildings in the middle of the winter. Later, trying to figure out the least violent method for the plan, Wenderoth and Philip decided that it would be impossible to put it into action without injuring some innocent person. The idea was rejected. It was one of any number of half-baked ideas that occur to people engaged in resistance and who are continually frustrated by their inability to achieve their goals. But in Lewisburg, where loneliness and isolation were having their effect on Philip the Washington tunnel scheme came back to mind and he made the catastrophic error of discussing it with Douglas. In the hands of the FBI, this revelation was dynamite.

When a letter from Elizabeth to Philip mentioned that William Stringfellow "will somehow be mixed up with bruv [their code name for Daniel]," the FBI wasted no time in putting a watch on Stringfellow's Block Island home. So it was that Daniel had been captured. Boyd Douglas was given a one-hundred-fifty-dollar bonus for the information. Another item in one of Elizabeth's letters led to the arrest of a group of draft resisters in Rochester, New York. But neither Elizabeth nor Philip ever connected these events with their own correspondence until months later when Director Hoover lowered the boom. So the stream of letters back and forth continued with the FBI scrutinizing each one for further information.

Daniel's capture and the arrest of the Rochester group brought the Catholic resistance community to a low point in their morale. Many of the best people were behind bars, the pace of the antiwar actions had slowed almost to a halt. On August 17, a plan was discussed to escalate once more the tactics of the resistance and bring the spotlight of national attention back to the antiwar movement. Eqbal Ahmad, furious that Daniel had disregarded his advice against staying with friends, called a meeting of Catholic activists at his wife's parents' home in Connecticut. Present were Elizabeth, Sister Jogues Egan, a close friend of the Berrigans, Paul Mayer, a member of the Milwaukee Fourteen, William Davidon, later named as a coconspirator, and Eqbal Ahmad, highly regarded among Catholic activists. A native of East

Pakistan (now Bengladesh), as a young child he had witnessed the murder of his mother and father because of their activity in land reform; he had also been in Algeria during the revolution there. One of the lessons he had learned was to be wary of imprisoned members of one's revolutionary group: "Send him oranges!" was the watchword, meaning, "Don't communicate anything important to him." Unfortunately this advice was not applied to Philip. When Ahmad began laying out the plan, the group listened with interest.

The meeting lasted most of the day. When Elizabeth McAlister sent her next letter to Philip she included a long description of the discussion. She wrote: "Eq outlined a plan for an action. . . . To kidnap—in our terminology to make a citizen's arrest of—someone like Henry Kissinger. Him because of his influences as a policymaker. . . ." The idea, she went on, was to hold him captive long enough to "hold a trial or grand jury affair" with prominent liberal critics of the war asking Kissinger questions on the conduct and long-range plans and goals of the war in Indochina. The hope was that Kissinger, out of fear for his own safety, would give away information on U.S. policy that was not publicly known. Another part of the plan was to make a film of the "trial." Demands would be made in return for Kissinger's release, such as a complete bombing halt and the release of political prisoners. "There is no pretense of the demands being met," Elizabeth wrote, "and he would be released after this time with a word that we're non-violent as opposed to you who would let a man be killed—one of your own kind—so that you can go on killing." Elizabeth suggested that at least Kissinger's role in the war would be impeded. Elizabeth urged him to think about it and let her know his opinion. At the close of the letter she explained why she had taken the risk of confiding the plan to paper— "to give you confidence that people are seriously thinking of escalated resistance."

It was a great risk, and as it turned out a foolish mistake, to write down the outline of what had gone on at the Connecticut meeting and send it into a prison where the chances were good that it would fall into the hands of government authorities. But for Elizabeth, the need to inform Philip of developments in the movement was greater than the risks. She had known for a long time that Philip was depressed over the state of the movement, and his inactivity in prison was increasing his gloom. Despite their vows as priest and nun of strict celibacy, they had come to love each other—a love that was very difficult to maintain across the high, thick walls of Lewisburg and the strength of their religious vows. The least Sister McAlister felt she could do was give Philip confidence that there were still people in the outside world as concerned and dedicated as he.

The letter from Elizabeth concerning the Kissinger plan was the last she was to send via Boyd Douglas. The efforts of Senator Goodell and others to have Philip transferred from Lewisburg to a minimum security prison had succeeded and he was scheduled to be moved to Danbury on August 25 where he would join Daniel. But Elizabeth's letter had concerned and stimulated Philip and he worked quickly to get out a reply via Douglas before the transfer.

His letter was highly critical of the idea of even a "nonviolent" kidnapping. ". . . the first time opens the door to murder," he wrote. He mentioned the Tupamaros of Uruguay, a guerrilla group that had pulled off several successful kidnappings but at a great cost to themselves in pitched battles with the police. Once we are forced to use violence against the state, he warned, they will not hesitate to use it against us. There were other objections as well. Kissinger was regarded by many as the liberal author of a plan to end the war, and was considered a healthy alternative to the other members of Nixon's staff.

Philip also doubted they would be able to get important

information out of the captured diplomat. "Nonetheless," Philip wrote, "I like the plan. . . ." Setting aside the objections he had already raised, Philip brought up the heating tunnels again. How about coordinating the kidnapping with a disturbance in the tunnels? Philip told Elizabeth to see Douglas for more information, or Joe Wenderoth or Neil McLaughlin, another radical priest. "It can be done and brilliantly," Philip said in closing.

It was a strange letter. As friends of Philip have pointed out, it was written in a period of crisis. Philip, desperate enough to risk committing such thoughts to paper, was seizing at fantasies. He gave the letter to Douglas and spent some time saying good-bye to the young man who had created a channel of communication for him when things were darkest. The next day he was driven to Danbury. It was the last time he was to see Boyd Douglas until the trial, when the informant appeared on the stand as the government's key witness and chief source of evidence.

Douglas took the letter and dutifully made a copy for the FBI before handing it over to Elizabeth. Impressed by Philip's views on the scheme, Elizabeth then copied the letter herself and gave it to Fathers McLaughlin and Wenderoth. They were outraged that Philip had been informed of the plan in the first place and doubly angry that he had sent a written response to it. They immediately burned the copy. When Sister Jogues Egan went to Danbury to visit Philip, Joe Wenderoth asked her to give him a message. "Hit him in the mouth for me!" he said. Sister Egan, who understood, nodded.

Philip's letter created a stir among his friends. It could very easily have created a lot of trouble, they thought, and it had also misconstrued much of what had originally been discussed in Connecticut. Eqbal Ahmad had never even used the term "kidnap." His wording was "citizen's arrest," actually a legally recognized act. Despite the emphasis on the nonviolent aspect of the plan, some of Berrigan's circle had been shocked, and after further discussion the plan was written off as unacceptable. Some days after Philip's final letter from Lewisburg, Elizabeth received a note from Douglas in which he showed a great deal of interest and enthusiasm for the plan and asked what he could do to help. This note Elizabeth destroyed. As far as the Catholic resistance and Eqbal Ahmad were concerned, there was nothing more to be said about it, and the plan was slowly forgotten. The FBI, however, was not so willing to forget.

11

With Philip no longer at Lewisburg, the FBI lost its direct line to the radical activities of the Catholic Left. But Douglas, who had managed to convince many other activists of his sincerity, continued gathering incriminating evidence for his employers. Through Elizabeth, he attempted to set up a meeting between himself and Eqbal Ahmad, who he assumed was at the center of the conspiracy to kidnap Kissinger. Elizabeth, however, was worried about Douglas's discretion, and never relayed the message to Ahmad.

On September 7, police apprehended a group of Catholic activists inside a draft board in Rochester, New York. The leads on the raid had been furnished by the FBI, which had received the information from Douglas. The Rochester group, which called itself "The Flower City Conspiracy," was the last in a long line of activists betrayed by Boyd Douglas. The informant made one last attempt to find out about the "kidnapping plot." Over a late breakfast with Elizabeth on September 26, Douglas made small talk about his plans after prison, but it was clear to Elizabeth he had something else on his mind. Eventually it came out. How were things going with the Kissinger project? Boyd wanted to know. No one else at that point was mentioning the discarded idea, except Douglas. Elizabeth made it clear that she didn't know and didn't care. It was the last mention of the old plan that anyone on the Catholic Left heard until the storm broke on November 27.

Appearing before a closed session of Senator Robert Byrd's Senate Appropriations Subcommittee, J. Edgar Hoover was presenting the reasons for an increase of a thousand agents for the FBI. Hoover, who rarely made such appearances himself, ran through a list of the problems faced by his department in preserving the internal security of the country. He mentioned the Weatherman group of the SDS, the Black Panthers, and then turned to a new terrorist threat that his department had uncovered.

Willingness to employ any type of terrorist tactics is becoming increasingly apparent among extremist elements. One example has recently come to light involving an incipient plot on the part of an anarchist group on the east coast, the so-called "East Coast Conspiracy to Save Lives."

This is a militant group, self described as being composed of Catholic priests and nuns, teachers and students and former students who have manifested opposition to U.S. participation in the Vietnam conflict.

The principal leaders of this group are Philip and Daniel Berrigan, Catholic priests presently incarcerated in the Federal Correctional Institution at Danbury, for their participation in the destruction of Selective Service records in Baltimore in 1968.

The group plans to blow up underground electrical conduits and steam pipes serving the Washington, D.C. area in order to disrupt Federal government operations. The plotters are also concocting a scheme to kidnap a highly placed Government official. The name of a high White House staff member has been mentioned as a possible victim. If successful, the plotters would demand an end to U.S. bombing operations in Southeast Asia and the release of all political prisoners as ransom. Intensive investigations are being conducted concerning this matter.

A few Washington reporters assigned to cover these hearings were sitting around the pressroom outside the committee chambers waiting for a routine press release. When the transcripts of Hoover's remarks arrived, the reporters leafed through them until one let out a long, low whistle and sat bolt upright in his chair. He called out the page number referring to the Berrigans. Within seconds they were all on the phone to their papers, telling their editors to hold the front page for a big story.

Within an hour after Hoover had finished his testimony, his allegations were being broadcast around the country as the number-one news item of the hour. Newspapers and magazines played the story up for all it was worth: CATHOLIC GUERRILLAS! HIGH WHITE HOUSE AIDE TO BE KIDNAPPED! BOMBS IN THE CAPITOL! The story was tailor-made for scare headlines.

Neil McLaughlin and Joe Wenderoth, the two priests who had been in on the citizen's arrest discussions, were at work painting the house they shared in Baltimore's ghetto when the news came over the radio. They were puzzled at first. "The East Coast Conspiracy," of which Wenderoth had been a member, had destroyed files in a draft board months earlier but had since disbanded. Philip and Daniel had had no connection with the group whatsoever, except as sources of inspiration. And, of course, there never had been any plot. Joking with each other about Hoover's paranoia, they went back to work. They both knew Douglas and liked and trusted him, and neither had any idea of the correspondence between Philip and Elizabeth. When Elizabeth appeared at their house in a state of shock, the two priests were surprised.

Elizabeth had first heard the news over her car radio while driving home after the Thanksgiving weekend, and had been stunned at Hoover's accusations. Her thoughts turned to Douglas and she wondered whether the FBI could possibly know anything about the smuggled letters. Douglas's questions about the Kissinger affair had annoyed her, yet she still did not distrust him. Listening to the radio broadcasts for three hours, Elizabeth finally decided to share her fears with her friends, McLaughlin and Wenderoth. The priests tried to calm her down, assuring her that Hoover couldn't possibly have any sound basis for his contentions. If he did, they reasoned, why hadn't they all been indicted?

When Eqbal Ahmad returned to New York from a Paris antiwar conference, he found Elizabeth still worried. Ahmad had never heard of Douglas. Sister Jogues Egan knew of the correspondence and had warned Elizabeth about trusting the convict. When Sister Egan told Ahmad he was outraged.

At Danbury prison, on a cold and snowy evening, Daniel and Philip heard Hoover's accusations on the late news. To avoid being overheard they walked to the handball court, pacing back and forth as they attempted to make sense out of the FBI director's statement. As Philip remembered that evening, "a ponderous gloom invaded us." At stake for Philip was the possibility of life imprisonment if the government took the conspiracy case to trial and convicted them. The man who had already been in prison for a total of a year and a half wondered how many more years he would spend there. He bitterly, but briefly, reflected that those who had avoided the issues he was in prison for were living out their lives unhindered.

Publicly, Daniel and Philip reacted with indignation at Hoover's accusations. Through their attorneys they released a statement the day after Hoover's Senate testimony. "At Danbury," the statement read, "we have neither the facilities nor the personnel to conduct such an enterprise. Nor do we have access to government funds. We have already been tried and condemned by Mr. Hoover's remarks, and we should have an opportunity to answer his charges . . . in view of the seriousness of the allegations he has made, he ought to prosecute us or publicly retract the charges he has made."

Many liberal papers echoed the same challenge—indict them or retract. Congressman William Anderson of Tennessee, the former commander of the submarine *Nautilus*, which had made headlines in the late fifties by sailing underneath the north pole, had become interested in the Berrigan brothers. A former advocate of a strong U.S. presence in Indochina, Anderson had become an opponent of the war. The congressman had met with the brothers at Danbury and been impressed by their candor and seriousness. On November 30, he rose in the House of Representatives and read an open letter to Hoover. Describing the Berrigans' commitment to nonviolence, the congressman said: "Seldom do men of such giant intellectual capacity come along. Even more rarely do we see men so committed to the poor, the oppressed and the victims of war as to purposefully risk imprisonment in order to project and dramatize their beliefs." Anderson asked Hoover to indict them before the grand jury if Hoover believed there was any substance to the allegations he had made.

With Daniel's and Philip's public statement, followed by Representative Anderson's demand and angry editorials in many newspapers, Hoover was forced to ask the Justice Department to convene a federal grand jury to hear the charges of conspiracy. Many of Hoover's own staff were unhappy about having the issue forced so soon. Hoover had jumped the gun with his Senate testimony. The agents working on the case felt there was insufficient evidence to convict anyone.

The grand jury indictment came with unusual swiftness. Early on the evening of January 12, 1971, Attorney General John Mitchell announced that six persons had been indicted on charges of plotting to blow up heating systems under federal buildings in the nation's capital and to kidnap Presidential Advisor Henry Kissinger. In addition, two of the defendants, Philip Berrigan and Elizabeth McAlister, were charged with seven counts of exchanging concealed communications at a federal penitentiary. The Justice Department's press release noted that five of the defendants had been arrested and the sixth, Philip Berrigan, was already in custody.

The arrests had come suddenly and without warning. Anthony Scoblick, a Josephite priest who had recently married without Vatican dispensation, was one of eight Boston Catholics who had destroyed draft records at three Boston Selective Service offices the previous February and joined Elizabeth McAlister, Joe Wenderoth, and others in the raid on four Delaware draft boards some months later. Scoblick's involvement in the so-called conspiracy was limited to his close friendship with the other defendants. He knew Boyd Douglas and had had many conversations with him on the nature and value of resistance. This was enough for the grand jury to name him in the indictment. It was a little after 6:00 P.M. on January 12, when Tony and his wife Mary heard a knock on the door. Scoblick went downstairs to see who it was. Opening the door, he was greeted by two men in business suits who smiled and inquired if he was Anthony Scoblick. Scowling through his horn-rimmed glasses, Scoblick nodded and asked who they were and what they wanted. In a rapid-fire voice one of the men read the substance of the indictment that had been handed down by the grand jury in Harrisburg, Pennsylvania, that afternoon. Identifying themselves as FBI agents, they walked into the house and informed Scoblick that he was under arrest. Ordering him to sit down, the two agents began to search the house.

Mary Cain Scoblick, a short, pretty woman, was upstairs waiting for Tony to call up and tell her who was there. When he didn't, she went down to see. She found her husband sitting in a chair, looking tired and depressed. Mary immediately realized the two men in her living room were FBI agents. They asked her to sit down as well. She refused and demanded to see their identification. They showed her their cards. She then asked if they had a warrant. One of the men calmly replied that no warrant was necessary—a bench warrant issued at Harrisburg was sufficient. The agents told Tony to stand up and then handcuffed him and led him outside to their car. Helplessly, Mary looked on.

Down the street from the Scoblick house, Fathers Wenderoth and McLaughlin were arrested moments later. Mary Scoblick had called them as soon as her husband was taken away and they told her to come right over, but when she arrived the house was empty.

The same afternoon, Sister Elizabeth McAlister was just leaving a lawyer's office in Newark, New Jersey, when she and two friends, Sister Jogues Egan and William Cunningham, one of the defense attorneys for the Catonsville Nine, were stopped by three men. Calling Elizabeth "Sister Liz," one of the men informed her that she was under arrest. Cunningham asked about a warrant and received the reply about the bench warrant in Harrisburg. Elizabeth embraced Sister Egan and Cunningham and was led away. As she walked to the agents' car she realized that there were seven other cars in the parking lot, all filled with FBI men. During the drive the agents continued to call her "Liz" and "Sister Liz," though she pointedly told them that her name was Elizabeth and that only her friends called her "Liz."

Eqbal Ahmad was in his office at the Adlai Stevenson Institute in Chicago that afternoon. Two FBI agents walked into the room and moments later came out with Ahmad between them. Calmly, Ahmad told his secretary to call his wife, for he'd been arrested. His secretary stared at him, then at the men with him. "Who's arrested you?" she asked.

"The FBI," Ahmad replied. "The FBI has arrested me."

"But what for?" his secretary persisted. Turning to the agent next to him, Ahmad asked him what he had been arrested for. Conspiracy, the agent told him.

"Conspiracy to do what?" Eqbal Ahmad asked.

"Conspiracy to kidnap a high government official," the agent replied, using the term originally employed by his chief, J. Edgar Hoover.

Turning back to his secretary, Ahmad repeated to her: "Conspiracy to kidnap a high government official."

The trio then left the room.

In Hoover's original statement he had named Philip *and* Daniel Berrigan as the ringleaders of the plot. But the government had nothing whatsoever on Daniel. In the indictment handed down at Harrisburg, those actually charged with the conspiracy were Philip, Elizabeth, Ahmad, Scoblick, Wenderoth, and McLaughlin. Daniel, along with Sister Jogues Egan and five others, was named a "coconspirator," an accessory to the conspiracy who was not to be charged with the crime. As it developed, the government could not substantiate that charge, but in a surprise move, Guy Goodwin, a lawyer in the Internal Security Division of the Justice Department who acted as commander and director of all federal grand juries in 1971, announced that the Harrisburg grand jury would not disband, but would continue the investigation and seek more indictments. What it amounted to was a "fishing expedition." The government was hoping, through the issuance of subpoenas to friends of the defendants, to gather more information for more indictments. This work was to last many months before anyone was actually brought to trial.

A grand jury is not like the jury at a regular trial. Called by the government to hear evidence on criminal activity, the grand jury is empowered to determine if the prosecution—in this case the federal government—has a case. If they decide positively, then an indictment is written up in the name of the grand jury and those named in it are arrested. Grand jury sessions are held behind closed doors. Only the prosecutor, the witness, the jury, and court officers are present. Because witnesses must answer questions without the presence of their attorney, the process is mysterious and intimidating.

On April 20, when the Harrisburg grand jury reconvened, federal agents served twenty-five subpoenas, summoning suspects or witnesses to appear. The questions asked by William Lynch, who took over as government prosecutor, went beyond the question of "conspiracy." The government tried to elicit information about all the draft board raids. In their "fishing expedition" the government was casting its net far, in the hope of catching all those even remotely connected with the Catholic resistance movement on the East Coast.

To their dismay, virtually all summoned refused to testify. Sister Jogues Egan rejected the repeated pleas of the judge and prosecutor Lynch to testify about her connections with her friends, the defendants. Offered immunity from prosecution for anything she might tell the jury, Sister Egan still refused. "I have no desire to be in contempt," she told the court, "but I have a duty to obey my conscience and a court which, I respectfully submit, is higher than this court." The judge then cited her for contempt of court and she was led away by federal marshals. Fortunately for Sister Egan, four days later a federal court heard her appeal and released her on her own recognizance.

Boyd Douglas kept his whereabouts a secret throughout the year-long investigation conducted by the grand jury. Most of the defendants, however, bore him little ill will. Philip, who had been closest to the informant, remarked, "I just feel sorry for him, that's all." Douglas's testimony was the great unknown element in the coming trial. Defense lawyers made repeated motions to be informed of his whereabouts, but the presiding judge, R. Dixon Herman, refused to require the government to say.

A hush settled on the grand jury proceedings as the government sent out its steady but futile stream of subpoenas. Even Eqbal Ahmad's in-laws were called to Harrisburg to testify. The government wanted them to confirm the meeting that had taken place in their Connecticut home the previous August, but this was impossible because they had been out of the country at the time.

On April 30, the government attempted to infuse new life into the case. The Justice Department announced a new indictment, superseding the old one. In essence there was little change, but the new indictment was phrased in terms that could make conviction easier to obtain. The first indictment, carrying life sentences, was now inoperative. Conviction on the second indictment would mean lesser prison terms, but the number of offenses had been expanded to include conspiracy to destroy draft records. Also, two new defendants were added: Mary Scoblick and Ted Glick, a member of the original East Coast Conspiracy to Save Lives and already a convicted draft board raider. Daniel Berrigan's name was not included in the new indictment, however.

During the grand jury proceedings that followed the first indictment, Tony Scoblick decided to take his case to the people. Draped in a blanket, he sat on the steps of the federal courthouse for several weeks, passing out leaflets to whoever would take one. The leaflets denounced the grand jury proceedings as an attempt by the government to stifle all opposition to the war. When the new indictment named Mary Scoblick as a defendant, she added her name to the leaflet.

To the Catholic activists the onslaught of government charges came as a terrible blow. Whereas in the trial of the Catonsville Nine, the defendants had chosen the ground for their battle, the case of the Harrisburg Seven was the other way around. This time the government was on the offensive. The money needed for bail, lawyers, and court costs severely hampered the ongoing work of the resistance. With the issuance of the second indictment it appeared that Catholic activists would have to fight for their very right to exist as a dissident element on the American political spectrum. The Harrisburg Defense Committee, which had been formed at the time of the original indictment, issued a statement by the defendants: ". . . instead of acknowledging the implausibility of the original kidnapping and bombing conspiracy charges, they now try to bury them in a general assault upon resistance efforts."

The government seemed bent on putting all the defendants away for a long time. In the second indictment, the possible prison terms for Elizabeth and Philip for smuggling letters in and out of Lewisburg were increased. Each charge carried with it a minimum of five years and a maximum of ten should the court find them guilty. Never before had anyone been tried for this offense. Any penalty for breaking prison laws is traditionally handled by prison authorities. But Philip and Elizabeth faced the possibility of serving forty years each if convicted on each count of smuggling.

After the grand jury was finally disbanded and pretrial motions were concluded, the trial began on January 24, 1972. Fourteen months had elapsed since the first accusation by Hoover.

On the morning of the first day of the trial, Philip Berrigan, handcuffed, a heavy link chain around his ankles, was led into the courtroom fifteen minutes before the court convened. Despite the shackles, he walked proudly erect and smiling. As was to be her custom every day of the two-month trial, Sister Elizabeth McAlister stood at the defendants' table to greet him. Smiling and talking quietly to each other, they stood close until the judge entered the room and rapped his gavel.

From the very first day it was clear that, unlike the trial of the Catonsville Nine, each point on the government's indictment was to be hotly contested by the defense. Selection of the jury took eleven days. The defense counsels voiced vigorous objections when a prospective juror indicated he might already have formed an opinion in the case. The jury eventually empaneled by the judge consisted of nine women and three men. One of them, a Catholic, was opposed to the war. Another was the mother of four conscientious objectors.

To represent them, the defendants had assembled a crew of well-known lawyers: Tom Menaker, a local Harrisburg attorney, chief counsel; William Cunningham, the Jesuit attorney who had worked on the Catonsville defense; Leonard Boudin, a prominent civil liberties lawyer; Paul O'Dwyer from New York, a silver-haired Irishman with immense eyebrows; Terry Lenzner, a young lawyer who had worked at the Office of Economic Opportunity; and Ramsey Clark, Attorney General of the United States during the last years of the Johnson administration. When he was Attorney General, Clark's name had appeared on the federal indictment of the Catonsville Nine. He had also been the author of the government conspiracy case against Dr. Benjamin Spock and four others. But when asked by Eqbal Ahmad about his supression of the antiwar movement, Clark had answered simply: "I was wrong."

On the other side of the room sat the government's prosecutor and his assistants. All were Catholics. William Lynch, the chief prosecutor, was proud of the second indictment, for which he had been responsible. He had assured reporters that there was no way for the defendants to wriggle out of the government's case.

Because of the enormous publicity the trial had stimulated, the press section was filled with reporters from around the country, including a handful of correspondents from foreign papers. Each day the reporters filed detailed stories on the proceedings, pitting the nonviolent Catholic Left against the entire legal and investigative machinery of the United States.

In the opening motions of the trial, Ted Glick requested permission to defend himself without an attorney. Judge Herman granted the request, but severed Glick's case from the others'. Leonard Boudin then asked the judge to separate Eqbal Ahmad's case, too, stating that there was evidence that the jury might be prejudiced against him because he was a foreigner involved in an internal security case. Ahmad, with his dark complexion, black hair, and large brown eyes, one of which had been injured and gave some the impression he could not look them in the eye, was very much the image of the "foreigner." But the judge denied the motion.

After the opening statements by the prosecution and the defense, the government called its first in a long line of witnesses. A parade of FBI agents, policemen, and prison officials filed to the stand over the first four days. They gave testimony about draft board raids and named some of the present defendants as participants in them. The warden of Lewisburg prison testified that he had allowed Douglas to carry the smuggled letters in and out of the prison. The government then called four women who had been well acquainted with Douglas at Bucknell. They had been granted immunity from prosecution by the judge, which forced them to testify, for if they refused they would be cited with contempt.

Smiling at the defendants as they took the stand, the four women grudgingly admitted to what they had already said to the grand jury. It didn't amount to much. Under defense questioning, however, the women revealed that while none of the defendants had ever suggested their participation in draft board raids, Douglas had actively tried to persuade them to.

One of the Bucknell women, a librarian who had taken an interest in Douglas because of his diligent studying in the library, was cited for contempt by Judge Herman when she attempted to read a statement denouncing the proceedings as a "black charade." After she was led away by a marshal, the judge directed prosecutor Lynch to call his next witness. Turning toward the door, Lynch announced in a loud voice: "Mr. Douglas!"

Every head in the room swiveled to the rear of the courtroom and, for a moment, there was total silence. No photographs of Douglas had appeared in the newspapers. His whereabouts had remained a state secret and Eqbal Ahmad, one of those implicated in Douglas's statements, had never even laid eyes on him.

The double doors swung open. Preceded by several deputy marshals, a short, pudgy man strode quickly down the aisle toward the stand. Douglas had gained a lot of weight since his release from prison in December, 1970. He had also changed his mode of dress from the unpretentious attire of his Lewisburg-Bucknell days to loud mod outfits. After being sworn in he sat down in the witness chair, his eyes never wavering from the lawyers at the prosecution table. Only once during his fifteen days of testimony, when he was asked to identify Elizabeth and Philip for the court, was Boyd Douglas forced to look in the direction of the defense table.

In his first day of testimony Douglas reviewed his relations with the defendants. He claimed both Philip and Father Joe Wenderoth had told him of a visit to the underground heating tunnels in Washington and mentioned the possibility of "getting at them." About the correspondence for which he had served as messenger, Douglas claimed that he had begun carrying the letters in innocence, claiming he was only helping a friend. Once he became aware that Philip was a hard-bitten revolutionary, Douglas said, he realized that sooner or later he would be discovered and would also be implicated in Philip's "plots." "I became concerned about the goals of these people," Douglas said. "I am a Catholic, and I am a product of a very strict Catholic upbringing. . . . I became concerned about what I was hearing from Father Philip Berrigan. . . . I felt that if I had enough evidence to produce at the time, the authorities would believe in what I was telling them . . . and they would realize the threats of these people to the United States government."

After two more hours of testimony that afternoon, the court adjourned. Douglas walked quickly out of the courtroom and, holding a newspaper over his face, got into a car filled with federal marshals.

Had the defendants known about Douglas's past, there would never have been a Harrisburg conspiracy trial. His parents having separated when he was a young child, Boyd had grown up with his father. But because he was constantly being accused of stealing by his teachers, the boy's father had sent him off to a reformatory where he fared no better. At the age of eighteen he was found guilty of passing bad checks and given the choice by the judge of either joining the army or going to jail. Stationed in Korea, he was a deserter three times in six months. The third time he was caught he was charged with impersonating an officer and passing a total of sixty thousand dollars' worth of bad checks. While serving his term at Lewisburg, he was a volunteer in an experimental medical program from which he suffered a bad reaction. Large abscesses developed on his arms and legs and he had to undergo a series of twenty-three operations. He then brought suit against the U.S. government for medical malpractice. After his parole in 1966, he went back to check fraud as a way of life and was once again apprehended. This time he made an attempt at suicide when he was reincarcerated. At his trial he pleaded that the pain from his abscesses had driven him to go on with his criminal spree. But he failed to convince the judge and was given a five-year sentence. It was during this last sentence that Douglas met Philip at Lewisburg.

At that point Douglas was passing himself off as a veteran of Vietnam and insisted to all who would listen that he was in jail for attempting to blow up a trainload of napalm. Either the Catholic activists badly wanted to believe him or he was a tremendously skillful liar. Most likely it was a combination of the two. After the trial, Philip wrote of Douglas: ". . . my compulsion fed his; his mine. Out of their union came the Harrisburg indictment."

Douglas returned to the witness stand the next morning, and continued to weave the threads of the government's case. But aside from those meetings already attested to by the other witnesses, the government could furnish no corroboration for most of Douglas's charges. The major piece of evidence was still the letters themselves. Lynch finally guided the questioning to Douglas's role as courier and the letters were introduced as evidence. One by one, Lynch read them to the court.

For Elizabeth and Philip, it was agonizing to hear their words read aloud in the courtroom. Much of the correspondence was intensely personal and had no bearing on the case, but the judge insisted it be heard in its entirety. This took most of the day and put some of the jurors, a marshal, several reporters, and two of the defendants to sleep. But when Lynch came to the proposed kidnapping, the courtroom came to life again. Pausing frequently to ask Douglas to clarify some of the references, Lynch elicited that Joe Wenderoth had been given two manuals on explosive charges. Douglas also stated that even after Hoover's charges were made public the kidnapping-bombing plot was still under discussion by the activists. Nevertheless, there was no evidence to back it up.

On the last day of direct examination by the prosecutors, Lynch asked Douglas about a letter he had written to the FBI asking for a large sum of money to continue his work. Douglas admitted writing it, and, smiling weakly, gave the figure: $50,000. The letter was already in the court's possession and the defense attorneys were aware of its contents. But when Paul O'Dwyer asked Lynch to read the letter aloud Lynch flatly refused. The jurors looked from the prosecutor to the witness to the judge, for a new and important question had been raised: Had Douglas been attempting to blackmail the FBI?

Judge Herman, whose sympathies seemed to lie with the government, ruled that Lynch could read the letter or not, whatever he pleased. But Lynch was aware of the intense curiosity Douglas's remarks had provoked, and he elected to read the letter. Whereas he had read the Philip-Elizabeth letters painfully slowly, he rushed through Douglas's letter so fast it was impossible to understand it. O'Dwyer leaped to his feet demanding that Lynch slow down, but Herman insisted that Lynch was reading it at the same rate as the others. "No, that isn't so!" persisted O'Dwyer.

Lynch made the mistake of reading so fast that the jury now was even more interested in its contents than before. Reading at a normal speed, Lynch continued: "Considering what I will go through before and after the trial . . . I request a minimum reward of $50,000 (tax free). . . ." Douglas looked down at the floor as the letter was read. The young man who had sat erect and confident for the past six days now looked dejected. "This figure doesn't account for expenses between now and the time of the trial," the letter went on. There was also a note of worry in it. He feared reprisal from those he was betraying, if not from the non-violent Catholics from "other types of people in the movement." When Lynch finished reading the letter, two of the jurors looked at each other and shook their heads.

As quickly as he could, Lynch switched the subject. But the damage had been done. After a few more questions concerning Douglas's relation to the antiwar Catholics after his release from prison, Lynch announced that the prosecution had no further questions. Now it was the defense lawyers' turn.

Douglas's seventh day on the stand began with a number of hard questions from Ramsey Clark. After establishing that it was Douglas who had suggested he be used as a "double agent" by the government, Clark went down the list of Douglas's convictions and activities over the past ten years. Then, displaying an Esso oil map of Washington, Clark pointed out that the underground heating tunnels beneath the official buildings were clearly marked on it and that it was available at any Esso station. Going further, Clark suggested that Douglas had made up the story about Philip and Wenderoth visiting the tunnels. Douglas denied this vehemently, and Clark announced he had no further questions. Paul O'Dwyer then began his cross-examination. O'Dwyer first drew Douglas out on the subject of the letter he had sent to the FBI demanding money. Douglas admitted that the idea of asking for a large sum came to him after he had received fifteen hundred dollars for information that led to the arrest of the Rochester draft board raiders. O'Dwyer went on to question Douglas on the amounts he had received from the FBI after he left prison. Slowly and with obvious reluctance, Douglas answered each question. He claimed to have received a total of almost ten thousand dollars from the government since that time.

O'Dwyer then asked the witness about his relationship with Betsy Sandel, a student at Bucknell whom Douglas had wooed and proposed to. Douglas had already admitted attending a meeting with FBI agents at which he had identified Catholic activists and Bucknell people in photographs. Betsy Sandel, he assured O'Dwyer, was one of those pointed out. Looking at the jury, O'Dwyer then asked Douglas if he had asked Betsy to marry him. Douglas blushed and answered, "Yes."

"Was it before or after you pointed out her picture to the FBI?"

His head bent toward the floor, Douglas mumbled, "I don't recall." It was the most devastating question asked yet of Boyd Douglas. Defense questioning had revealed Douglas's total lack of character. He now appeared to the jury to be a person completely lacking in scruples. He had lied to his own employers, the FBI, on certain matters, tried to extort money from them, and had proposed to a woman on whom he was actually spying.

After O'Dwyer had finished with Douglas, the rest of the defense table tore into Douglas's testimony. Terry Lenzner questioned Douglas on letters he had written to students at Bucknell, describing himself as "a militant dedicated to the movement" and asking them for the same commitment. Lenzner got Douglas to admit that he had attempted to recruit at least one student for civil disobedience. When Lenzner had finished, the jury could add the term *provocateur* (one who incites others to break the law) to Douglas's list of accomplishments.

When the defense attorneys had completed their cross-examination, Lynch was allowed to reexamine his witness. Attempting to salvage what was left of Douglas's character and evidence, Lynch insisted that ever since Douglas had left prison he had been a model citizen. But as Paul O'Dwyer pointed out from the defense table, the government had kept Douglas hidden away for the past year and a half under constant surveillance. Outflanked again, Lynch could make no response, except to insist feebly to the jury that Douglas was of "sterling character."

Douglas, the star witness for the prosecution, finally stepped down after fifteen days on the stand. It was now time for the defense to present its case. The evening before, the defendants and their lawyers had held a strategy meeting.

There was serious disagreement in the group as to whether or not a defense should be presented at all. Mary and Tony Scoblick, Neil McLaughlin, and Joe Wenderoth felt that the government's case against them was now so riddled with holes and falsehoods that the only honorable defense was one of silence. If the defendants called witnesses now, the faction argued, the government would only seize the opportunity to gather more information from them and possibly issue new indictments. Philip, Elizabeth, and Eqbal Ahmad saw it differently. So far, they argued, their defense had consisted of exposing the legal flaws in the government's case, and the question of politics had not been raised. All the jury knew of their political position, they argued, was what the government had told them, and the defendants had an obligation to inform the jurors about their moral and religious views and the reasons for their acts of civil disobedience. They could come to no agreement and a vote was taken. The next morning, when court reconvened, Ramsey Clark rose to say: "The defendants will always seek peace, the defendants continue to proclaim their innocence—and the defense rests." William Lynch looked over at the defense table, an expression of disbelief on his face. Some twenty-five witnesses had been subpoenaed already and everyone had expected a lengthy defense. The government's lawyers whispered furiously together. It was clear they suspected the defense was trying to put something over on them.

But the next day the summations began. Lynch delegated

the summing up of the government's case to a young assistant who described the defendants to the jury as a group of intelligent, crafty, well-educated people who had tried to use a high school drop-out, Boyd Douglas, for their nefarious purposes. The defense lawyers all took a turn before the jury. Paul O'Dwyer reread the sections of the letters that described Philip's and Elizabeth's feelings for each other and their religious and political outlooks. His lilting Irish voice left the jury spellbound. What had sounded sinister when read by the government prosecutor now seemed lyrical and moving and honest. Ramsey Clark was the last attorney to speak. At the end of his summation he told the jury: "If you believe Boyd Douglas you'll go to your last day wondering whether you were the most recent of a long, long line of people he has taken in."

There was confusion among the jurors on how to interpret both the indictments and the judge's instructions. They returned twice during sixty hours of deliberation to have the judge reexplain certain matters and reread portions of the law. On April 5, the jury announced that they had found Philip and Elizabeth guilty on three counts each of smuggling letters. But on the matter of the conspiracy charges, they were deadlocked. The judge was left with no alternative but to declare a mistrial. If the government chose to try the case again, the defendants would have to stand trial once more. In the meantime, they were free.

Publicly, Lynch and his cocounsels congratulated themselves for managing to convict Philip and Elizabeth, but otherwise the trial was a shattering defeat for the government. What had been portrayed as a vast conspiracy had fizzled into a handful of convictions for illegal letter passing. When Ronald Ostrow and Jack Nelson of the *Los Angeles Times* asked the new Attorney General, Richard Kleindienst, if the government had any intention of retrying the case, Kleindienst asked if they were "crazy." A few months after the trial, the government moved quietly to drop the conspiracy indictments.

In the weeks after the trial the Catholic resistance movement attempted to get back on its feet. The trial had absorbed much of its resources and over a year of its time, while the object of the struggle, the war in Vietnam, raged on. If the government's purpose had been to throw a monkey wrench into the antiwar movement, it had succeeded.

Between 1970 and 1972, dozens of other major trials took place around the country involving alleged conspiracies by groups of militants. The Bobby Seale trial in New Haven, the conspiracy trials of the Chicago Seven and the Panther Twenty-one were among those the government, by means of vaguely worded charges or poorly prepared cases, pressed against political resistance movements.

The overall effect, however, in the wake of the Harrisburg conspiracy trial, was that the American people were once again made aware of the injustices of life in America. For this the Harrisburg Seven could congratulate themselves.

12

In the opening weeks of the Harrisburg trial, Daniel Berrigan kept informed of the proceedings by radio, newspaper, and messages relayed through friends. To be cut off from his brother and the movement at that crucial time was a source of anguish to him. The conspiracy indictment, Daniel felt, was the government's attempt to crush the Catholic resistance movement. Without a loud outcry from the public, Daniel feared they might succeed.

The previous June a massive allergic attack had seriously impaired Daniel's health. At the time, Philip and some other Danbury inmates had petitioned the Connecticut Board of Parole to release Daniel but the board had rejected the petition. Daniel's health had improved somewhat since then, but he continued to have frequent allergic attacks that left him weak and disabled. Duing the winter, his health worsened again. In February, 1972, the parole board announced that Daniel would be released, citing his ill health. The ailing priest was overjoyed at the prospect of making the trip to Harrisburg. Released on February 24, Daniel arrived in Harrisburg by the end of the week. He was a daily spectator at the trial. Sitting just behind the defense table, he was able to carry on whispered conversations with Philip and the defendants. He immediately became active in the Harrisburg Defense Committee. When the jury retired to seek a verdict, Daniel was at the head of ten thousand people rallying in front of the courthouse demanding freedom for the Harrisburg Seven.

The marchers had come from all over the country, exhibiting the same militant fervor and anger they had displayed in the streets of Baltimore during the trial of the Catonsville Nine. Many of the demonstrators remained in the Pennsylvania capital awaiting the verdict. When the jury returned they held a big celebration.

The Harrisburg Defense Committee continued its work even after the trial ended. Philip and Elizabeth were intent on appealing their convictions for smuggling letters. The American Civil Liberties Union and a number of other lawyers around the country felt the convictions were of a vindictive nature—had it not been for the accompanying charges of conspiracy, the government would never have prosecuted. More than a year later, the appeals were successful and all convictions resulting from the Harrisburg trial were overturned.

While Philip remained in Danbury prison, serving out the rest of his original six-year term, Daniel busied himself with antiwar work. He was visibly older now, after his prison term and successive illnesses. Still boyishly slim and erect, Daniel seemed frailer and less immune to life's hazards. His dark hair was graying at the temples. Parole regulations, which were to last until August, 1973, restricted him to a radius of about two hundred miles around New York City, but within those borders he continued to agitate against the war and speak out against injustice. Alongside David Dellinger, a veteran New York peace activist, Daniel appeared at a news conference in August, 1972, announcing plans for a nonviolent march on the Republican National Convention in Miami later that month. "We're going to confront the administration that continues to make war on people in Indochina," Daniel told the press. He would love to be there himself, he added, but doubted his parole officer would appreciate it. In November, Daniel was part of a picket line in front of a hospital on Manhattan's Upper West Side, protesting the hospital's expansion plans, which were being carried out at the expense of the local community. He was busy writing as well and published two volumes of prose that fall: *America Is Hard to Find*, a collection of pieces written while underground, and *Absurd Convictions, Modest Hopes*, a transcript of long conversations held with the writer Lee Lockwood, also during the underground period. It was shortly after the release of those two books that a committee appointed by the Norwegian parliament announced that it had accepted the nomination of Daniel and Philip Berrigan for the Nobel Peace Prize. Writers in both Catholic and secular journals noted that the peace prize would be an appropriate and fitting honor for the two rebellious priests. But if they won the awards, Daniel would be unable to leave the United States because of his parole restrictions, and Philip would still be imprisoned at Danbury. It might be an embarrassing moment for the U.S. government, the writers suggested.

On November 30, the parole board made its monthly routine announcements concerning paroles granted and refused. Without commenting on the reasons, the board included the name of Philip Berrigan among paroles granted. The unexpected move by the parole board, which is selected by the Justice Department, made headlines across the nation. After serving thirty-eight months in prison, the controversial forty-nine-year-old priest was to be released.

About three hundred people stood in ankle-deep snow outside the walls of Danbury prison on December 20, 1972. There had been no widespread appeal for supporters to gather at that time and place. They had come of their own accord to show their respect and appreciation of the man they felt had given so much of himself on behalf of others. Chatting among themselves, and moving around to keep warm, the group kept an eye on the chain-link gate through which Philip Berrigan would soon pass. When he emerged, still a commanding figure even in the loosely fitting prison-made suit, they swarmed to meet him. Daniel was the first to reach him. Throwing their arms around each other, the brothers danced up and down in the snow while dozens of outstretched hands clapped the ex-convict on the back. Newsmen crowded around him for a statement, but before issuing it, Philip turned back toward the prison and with a clenched fist saluted the prisoners of Danbury, some of whom could be seen waving from the prison building. He had not been allowed to say Mass for the prisoners, yet they had sought him out on their own, as a priest and confessor, and as a wise and trusted friend. Standing beside him, Daniel, too, raised his arm in salute.

Photographers scurried about capturing a picture of the ex-convicts waving good-bye to their friends and former neighbors. When Philip turned back to the reporters his face was hard and angry. Prisons, he told the newsmen, "are laboratories of waste, injustice and despair." Daniel nodded in assent. Around his neck hung a cross made of two welded screws, a gift from a fellow prisoner. A half hour later, many of Philip's greeters gathered at an inn a few miles from the prison. There, amidst rejoicing, Philip held a brief Mass, his first in almost thirty-eight months.

There was much speculation in the media and among Catholic activists about the reasons for Philip's sudden release. The *New York Times* speculated in an editorial that the parole was part of a wide-ranging plan of the Nixon administration to defuse dissent across the country. But if the White House had hoped to pacify the rebellious Catholic Left by Philip's release it had acted in vain. Within days of his release, Philip was reminding the public in television interviews and press conferences that an enormous amount of work remained to be done if the country truly wished to live in peace. He also announced to his friends that he and Elizabeth McAlister would marry without receiving dispensation from their vows. It was one more unorthodox act by this most unorthodox priest. He and Daniel immediately sought permission from their parole boards to visit North Vietnam, which was then undergoing the most intense bombing attacks of the war. Refused by their boards, Philip and Daniel appealed the rulings to higher courts while holding constant press conferences. But the government refused to back down and no permission was granted.

In February, 1973, after the cease-fire in Vietnam had been signed, and the first American prisoners of war were being received with brass bands, jubilant crowds, lifetime passes to baseball games, and accolades from politicians, Philip Berrigan sounded one of the few somber notes. "One must be very much aware," he told reporters, "that these men have been destroyers." The comment was typical. Like ceaselessly tolling harbour buoys, Daniel and Philip Berrigan continue to sound their warnings. To their church, and to the people of their country, they are gadflies of conscience. This is part of their heritage as Christians and priests, they have said; they must confront wrongdoing and injustice wherever they find it. For they take literally the words of Christ to Pontius Pilate: "For this I was born, and for this have I come into the world, to bear witness to the truth."

BIBLIOGRAPHY

Berrigan, Daniel. *Absurd Convictions, Modest Hopes* Conversations with Lee Lockwood. New York: Random House, 1972.

————. *America Is Hard to Find.* New York: Doubleday & Co., 1972.

————. *The Bride.* New York: The Macmillan Company, 1959.

————. *The Bow in the Clouds.* New York: Coward, McCann & Geoghegan, Inc., 1961.

————. *Consequences: Truth and . . .* New York: The Macmillan Company, 1967.

————. *Encounters.* New York: World Publishing Company, 1960.

————. *The Geography of Faith: Conversations Between Daniel Berrigan, When Underground, and Robert Coles.* Boston: Beacon Press, 1971.

————. *Love, Love at the End: Parables, Prayers and Meditations.* New York: The Macmillan Company, 1968.

————. *Night Flight to Hanoi: Daniel Berrigan's War Diary with Eleven Poems.* New York: The Macmillan Company, 1968.

————. *No Bars to Manhood.* New York: Doubleday & Co., 1970.

————. *No One Walks Waters.* New York: The Macmillan Company, 1966.

————. *They Call Us Dead Men.* New York: The Macmillan Company, 1968.

————. *Time Without Number.* New York: The Macmillan Company, 1957.

————. *The Trial of the Catonsville Nine.* Boston: Beacon Press, 1970.

————. *The World for Wedding Ring.* New York: The Macmillan Company, 1962.

Berrigan, Philip. *A Punishment for Peace.* New York: The Macmillan Company, 1969.

————. *No More Strangers.* New York: The Macmillan Company, 1971.

————. *Prison Journals of a Priest Revolutionary*. New York: Ballantine Books, Inc., 1971.

Casey, William VanEtten, Nobile, Philip (eds.). *The Berrigans*. New York: Avon Books, 1970.

Forest, James. "Harrisburg Conspiracy: The Berrigans and the Catholic Left." *Win Magazine* 9 (1973): 3–31.

Gray, Francine duPlessix. *Divine Disobedience*. New York: Alfred A. Knopf, 1970.

Halpert, Stephen, and Murray, Tom (eds.). *Witness of the Berrigans*. New York: Doubleday & Co., 1972.

Nelson, Jack, and Ostrow, Ronald J. *The FBI and the Berrigans*. New York: Coward, McCann & Geoghegan, Inc., 1972.

O'Rourke, William. *The Harrisburg Seven and the New Catholic Left*. New York: Thomas Y. Crowell, 1972.

Windass, Stanley (ed.). *The Chronicle of the Worker-Priests*. New York: Humanities Press, 1967.

INDEX

INDEX